DR MICHAELA GLÖCKLER has been leader of the Medical Section at the Goetheanum, School of Spiritual Science in Dornach, Switzerland, since 1988. She attended the Waldorf School in Stuttgart, then studied German language, literature and history in Freiburg and Heidelberg. She studied medicine in Tübingen and Marburg and trained as a paediatrician at the community hospital in Herdecke and Bochum University Paediatric Clinic. She worked in the children's outpatient clinic at Herdecke and served as school doctor for the Rudolf Steiner School in Witten, Germany. Michaela has many publications in German, and is a co-author of *A Guide to Child's Health*.

MEDICINE AT THE THRESHOLD OF A NEW CONSCIOUSNESS

Michaela Glöckler

TEMPLE LODGE

Translated from the German

Temple Lodge Publishing
Hillside House, The Square
Forest Row, RH18 5ES

Published by Temple Lodge 1997
Reprinted 2013

Originally published in German by Verlag am Goetheanum, Dornach, Switzerland in 1993. Part One appears in *Sind wir überfordert?* and Part Two in *Medizin an der Schwelle*

© Verlag am Goetheanum 1993
This translation © Temple Lodge Publishing 1997

The moral right of the author has been asserted under the Copyright, Designs and Patents Act, 1988

All rights reserved. No part of this publication may be reproduced, stored in a retrieval system, or transmitted, in any form or by any means, electronic, mechanical, photocopying, recording or otherwise, without the prior permission of the publishers.

A catalogue record for this book is available from the British Library

ISBN 978 1 906999 49 0

Cover by Morgan Creative featuring logo of the Medical Section, Goetheanum, Switzerland
Typeset by DP Photosetting, Aylesbury, Bucks
Printed and bound by 4Edge Ltd., Essex

Contents

Foreword *by Jenny Josephson*   vii

Part 1

1. The Path of Development as a Therapeutic Task for the Individual   3

2. The Path of Development as a Therapeutic Task for the Community in Professional and Daily Life   17

3. The Path of Development as a Therapeutic Task for the Connection of the Individual with Humanity   34

Part 2

1. Medicine at the Threshold   51

   The Human Foundations of Science, Art and Religion   53

   From the Temple Sleep of the Egyptian Mysteries to the Hygienic Occultism of Today   57

   Ethical Questions as Threshold Questions   69
   (i)   Questions about organ transplantation   70
   (ii) Confusion in old age — standing at the threshold of death   76
   (iii) On the termination of pregnancy   79

   Symptoms of the Unconscious Crossing of the Threshold   86

   On the Renewal of the Mysteries   89

2. The Evolution of the Medical Section in
   Connection with the School for Spiritual Science
   at the Goetheanum   103

Notes   108

Foreword

This book arises out of two events held at the Goetheanum, Dornach under the aegis of the Medical Section. The first part comes from an international 'Curative Education and Social Therapy' conference held in 1992. Michaela Glöckler gave three lectures, which later formed the main part of a book, *Sind Wir Überfordert?* ('is too much asked of us?'). The quality of direct speech in these lectures is such that each and everyone of us is addressed personally in some part of our being. Curative education embraces most, if not all professions in some way or other and so these lectures have relevance for all of us, but particularly of course for those involved with some aspect of caring or healing.

One of the questions Michaela is often asked has to do with the inner content, the inner path of therapeutic activity. While each area must have its own content, these lectures can also help us to find the general aspects — especially if taken together with a meditative study of Rudolf Steiner's sculptural group, the 'Representative of Man'. The second part of the book comes from a General Medical Section conference held in 1991 at the Goetheanum for members of the 'School of Spiritual Science'.[1] These contributions, along with other contributors' lectures, talks etc., form part of another book, *Medizin an der Schwelle*, ('medicine on the threshold'). This conference also addressed a very broad range of disciplines, including those whose activity is not primarily medical but where medical activity is a conscious sub-heading. In these contributions the tone is not so much that of the inner doing, the inner path, but rather the application of it in our conscious, outer activity. How do we learn to ask the right questions? Where do we need to look? What are the particular areas where, out of an anthroposophical background and inner schooling, we can make a contribution not only to practical doing and healing but also to the consciousness of what is done? How do we contribute in a helpful way to medical ethics and through that, to the being and Mystery of medicine?

Although some of the material could appear to repeat itself, on closer reading and reflection it does not. For the direction taken is a different one in each different context; and though the same material is the starting point, the application varies: an example of open-mindedness and the fruitfulness of looking at things from much more than only one point of view!

In her first year as Section Leader, Michaela Glöckler was often asked about her intentions for the Medical Section and its structure and influence. She answered that the Section comes about wherever work is in progress. And to the question of a 'Section College', she replied that all those who take initiative—in the spirit of the General Anthroposophical Society and the Medical Section of the School of Spiritual Science—are members of this College. By the same token, both Section and College cease to be present if the work/initiative ceases.

In the meantime we have experienced that work and practice—both inner and outer, and at times in breathtaking intensity—has taken place and is a keynote of the Section. Another is Michaela's warmth, interest and good will for the efforts of others and her ability to see the opportunities for development in difficult or negative situations. In this she echoes the sentiments expressed in Ita Wegman's letter in the text.

Much has been achieved in the first nine years of Michaela Glöckler's leadership of the Medical Section; more is undoubtedly to come, but this book allows us to taste the flavour of the first years.

Jenny Josephson, Michaelmas 1997

Part 1

1
The Path of Development as a Therapeutic Task for the Individual[1]

One of the central tasks of the Medical Section at the Goetheanum is to make anthroposophy fruitful for an understanding of health and illness, and for developing an active will for helping, for learning how to help and for being able to help. This is the spiritual mission which we received from the founders of this Section—Rudolf Steiner and Ita Wegman.[2] Just as it is the overall task of the Goetheanum, as an independent 'School of Spiritual Science', to renew the Mysteries of ancient cultures in the spirit of Christianity, so is this particularly true for the Mysteries of Healing under the auspices of the Medical Section. The question of the path of development as a therapeutic task leads us into the centre of these Healing Mysteries. For what is physical and soul health?

Physical health allows the human being to use the body to assimilate everything that comes towards it as external influences—such as geology, climate and nutrition. Open senses, an alert ability to react, free play of the limbs and the possibility of movement: the body serves as an instrument of self-discipline and activity, as well as one for perceiving the world. It is the instrument for the tasks of earthly life.

It is good to understand why Rudolf Steiner continually and clearly makes the point that physical limitation or illness can be the destined consequence of disinterest in the world or the inability to assimilate experiences.[3] Illness thus becomes a picture of the incapacity of the human ego, or, expressed positively, a picture of a task to be learnt. It is a contradiction if the ego is on earth but does not interest itself in the world. One is there and yet not there, because one is not alert. One disassociates inwardly from the world, from earthly and life connections. This inner disassociation, this lack of active interest and wish to learn, then transforms itself in the life between death and rebirth into tendencies to illness in the next life on earth,[4] so that the human being can experience in his next life, in his own body, the consequences of his behaviour in the previous life on earth; through this, one can learn to know oneself better and to see one's task on earth in a new light.

Now there is also another group of illnesses—the psychological, soul, or mental and emotional illnesses. These too have a common root. They are the expression, the picture, of the fact that we did not interest ourselves sufficiently in others in our immediate or wider surroundings. If we withdraw inwardly from human social connections and are interested mainly in ourselves, with a corresponding disinterest in other people, then we actively prepare the soul disposition which subsequently arises in a later life as a tendency to illness, and which leads to being caught in our own soul, i.e. mental illness. To both physical and mental illness applies the principle that the ego's freedom and room for manouevre in one life becomes in the next a disposition to illness, to a soul or bodily state that does not leave one free but must be worked through.

The path of self-development since the oldest mysteries has always had only one goal: to bring human beings into the full possession of their archetypal powers; to give them full self-control and with that, the capacity to hold their own against the spiritual world and to bear being morally weighed in the balance by higher beings. One gained this inner power through schooling, and so the struggle for full self-control, i.e. for full health, has always been connected with the path to the spiritual world. It is our salvation and healing that we may learn to know ourselves as citizens of two worlds; it is our salvation and healing that we may open ourselves to the pure, good, stimulating, higher world of being that leads us on our further path of development.

Those for whom we care in curative-educational and social-therapeutic institutions, behave on earth as if they had at least partly remained in the spiritual world. When we so-called healthy people enter the spiritual world, we actually become completely handicapped ourselves, in need of special caring, placing ourselves with no will of our own into a new world situation, allowing ourselves to be led by the higher hierarchies through the course of the planetary spheres to world midnight and back into new life on earth.[5]

The way in which those we care for place themselves into the morning circle, at the breakfast table, in morning activities, in the artistic exercises, in school, in the whole regulated rhythm of day, week, month and year, we so-called healthy people do only in childhood and in the spiritual world. This gives rise to the very particular situation that exists in curative-educational and social-therapeutic institutions. Here, human souls are present who have not completely left the spiritual world: for karmic reasons this is how it is for them this time. This means that they experience the earth sphere from a spiritual aspect and expect us to be a bit like the higher beings, the hierarchies, who they know well and with whom they are still so strongly connected.

Institutions of this kind have only arisen in this century. Previously, medicine and therapy were embedded in family, village, country and folk circumstances. Healing was an innate faculty, passed on by the parents in certain families to their descendants. These instinctive healing forces and faculties were known, and little teaching was needed to use them. It was, in fact, an instinctive, semi-conscious art of healing that lived on from the old Mystery times, and was not a consciously chosen profession. When the first kinds of hospital arose in the monasteries in the Middle Ages, they were completely tied to conditions of the

Church; pedagogy also was purely a concern of the Church. This could well be a reason why many of the healing professions still do not feel entirely competent as yet and, as a result, are hit by so-called 'burn-out' syndrome. There are in fact many new professions which, besides the usual training, take much for granted. Every profession needs an adequate training in our present time. The most important thing, however, is usually not taught to either teachers or therapists nowadays: namely, how they can attain to true pedagogical and therapeutic faculties, i.e. become pedagogues and therapists.

It is a necessity of our present time that we concern ourselves now with this theme. Therapy, the loving devotion to someone in need of care, was something that up until the eighteenth-nineteenth century was performed by the family, and could be carried out because family connections were still experienced so strongly. One could devote oneself lovingly to caring for someone in need and to taking on their needs, because one knew them, because they were a brother or a sister. From blood-ties one drew the strength through which compassion and readiness to act arose. Today that is quite different! Families do not manage this any more—conditions and circumstances of life changed radically at the turn of the nineteenth to twentieth century. The individual now wrestles himself free from the family; young people leave their parents' house at an early age. They want to get away from blood-ties, out into the world, away from the village, away from the town, into homelessness! They want to find their ego, their personality. There is no longer a place for therapy working through blood-ties.

We have crossed a threshold to individuality, but also a threshold to the deepest loneliness—the threshold to exile, where we realise that no one helps us any more if we do not help ourselves. At the same time, we have actually also crossed the threshold to the spiritual world, inasmuch as each of us today experiences the need to take responsibility for ourselves and our surroundings. The carrying social structures that could relieve the individual of this burden are no longer there. The last remnants of the old Mystery knowledge in State, culture and Church, that were able to support and help externally, are drying up more and more, and are clearly experienced as being out of date. The individual feels with greater or lesser clarity: Everything must be found anew through the strength of the ego, which itself recollects its inner connection with the beings of the spiritual world, its spiritual home on the other side of the threshold dividing the world of the senses from the world of the spirit.[6] The threshold to the spiritual world projects into each human heart at the point where sense experiences meet with the spiritual-moral experiences of our thinking, feeling and willing.

There have been great pioneering attempts arising from both church and anthroposophical contexts, to create entirely new social-therapeutic institutions—there are many such models in the world today. Institutions in which people choose freely the profession of loving the other, make into a profession something that can only be attained through the forces of consciousness and schooling, in which family love is spiritualised into a general love for humanity. It is therefore understandable that we, as members of these professions, are often in the situation of leading double lives: on the one side are my personal needs, and on the other an intimation that this profession demands something quite different from what I need for myself. My profession demands that I grow beyond my limitations. But I must also maintain this tension of being true to myself and, despite this, growing beyond my limitations and becoming true to my work.

Then, inwardly, a third aspect silently begins to germinate: I am not only responsible for myself and my profession but I am at the same time a member of the whole of humanity. My body is taken from this earth, from all matter; I also breathe and digest the air that comes from industrial firms, from the Sahara and from the furthest regions of the earth. In terms of the physical body I am already a member of the whole, and I become ever more aware that I am also a member of the whole as soul and spirit, co-responsible for the destiny of humanity.

Today we seek this inner *conscious* connection to humanity as a whole, going beyond that of the bodily, inherited, unconscious experience of belonging. But we also experience powerlessness in that we do not succeed as a matter of course.

The ancient Mysteries gave people the possibility of entrusting themselves on earth to the guidance of the Mystery teachers. People trusted that these priests of the Mysteries—through initiation, later through the oracles—could receive the impulses, the guidelines, the orientating indications from the spiritual world for the forming of external life, even to the extent of bringing about war and peace. However, these old Mysteries presumed that contact with the spiritual world still existed—and we know that this was already gradually fading from 300 BC on. The spiritual world became more and more silent for seeking human beings and the last remnants of divine revelations were ultimately taken up into certain philosophical formulae and basic premises. This was like a farewell greeting from the old Mysteries. It then became spiritually dark for humanity and the time began, when, inspired by the appearance of Christ on earth, human beings began to learn independently, to give themselves their own direction and the social orientation that they needed and wanted. It was increasingly experienced that one's own thoughts, goals and ideals, which one was now permitted and able to develop for oneself, would enable one to find a new connection to the spiritual guiding forces emanating from higher beings, in particular Christ Himself—forces which can nowadays be taken up into human thinking as the image of human evolution's ultimate goal. Through personal seeking, in free, self-aware thinking, and no longer held back from access to one's own judgement by a Mystery priest. No, self-aware and in conscious connection with other human beings, opening oneself to the revelations of the spiritual world—this has become the new possibility of self-fulfilment, the starting point of a new Christian Mystery. In this sense, we experience the double aspect of our ego quite clearly: it unfolds its activity at first under outside guidance, unconscious of its own power, and in the course of development begins to recognise ever more clearly that it is called upon to direct itself. This is mirrored, correspondingly, in the development in childhood and youth of each individual.

The new Mysteries are of the ego. Everything that was revealed by the old Mysteries as unending wisdom, consisted, in fact, of revelations from the microcosmic image of the macrocosmos, i.e. from the astral and etheric body, from their immense wealth of wisdom, from their permeation and penetration by the workings of higher beings. Now everything must pass through the ego's eye of the needle, and this ego is, like Parzival,[7] at first 'stupid'—an immense force but as yet completely untrained, uneducated. The wisdom of one's own being must be consciously attained by the ego itself.

This ego being of man is the most valuable possession. It is like an uncut precious stone. Through our own impetus it enables us to attain, and work in a new way with, all the wisdom in the world, all the love in the world and all the power in the world. In its inner nature the ego is truth, love, and free will—just as it is written in the St. John's Gospel about the ego nature of the Christ; and, since we should make this our own, of us.

If we look at the human being of today, at what endangers us in our constitution, we can see that, unnoticed, the cultural conditions of our time are directly attacking this ego, this uncut precious stone, in order that at all costs the ego might not begin to shine, that it might not notice what it is! This process, this attack on the ego, has already advanced so far in the course of this century, that now, at the end of the century we can speak about a fourfold process of alienation that the ego has undergone. The symptoms of this fourfold alienation are known to us all; today I will therefore indicate them only briefly:

We can observe the alienation of the ego from the physical body wherever the physical body becomes dependent, where the ego does not have control over this body, where the body slips out of its grasp. Drug addiction can nowadays begin as early as the ninth year. The W.H.O. statistics show that if developments continue in this way—including the consumption of sleeping tablets and alcohol, not just hard drugs—every second person will, in some form, be drug-dependent by 2100.

A further area of alienation from the physical is the addiction to sexuality, in which sexuality is no longer the expression of a loving relationship between people, the greatest joy of experiencing spirit and body in complete unity. Instead, it becomes divorced from its meaning—becomes isolated self-enjoyment and making use of the other to experience oneself. It is reduced to bodily stimulation and sensuality for its own sake. Through this, the ego busies itself more and more with itself, does not identify with the knowledge of other human beings which can be won through bodily experience. It gets trapped in the body, thus alienating itself from the true purpose of this body, i.e. to be an organ of perception and mastery of self and world.

A third area is the superficiality of sense-perception. In what an uninterested and superficial way do we go through life today! Even when we make an effort, civilisation forces us to see far more than we can grasp and work through in a conscious and responsible way. Nowadays one must do observation exercises in order to maintain and school a quality of real awareness and attention. However, through this ego activity, through loving observation, we strengthen our ego in the physical body—from which, on the other hand, it is alienated through lack of attentiveness.

A further impulse of our civilisation consists in the tendencies which alienate the ego from the etheric organism.[8] We can observe routines, material compulsions, egoless habits everywhere. Something is done any old way, just because it has to be done. One does not engage in it with the full presence of the ego; stress and haste also rule many activities. Through this, the ether organisation wastes away and grows weak.

A third alienation—the ego from the astral—can be observed whenever we have wishes, tendencies, urges and longings within us which have no real chance of satisfaction. When we wish for something which we are quite sure cannot be realised, and yet still nourish this wish, then we are involved in the birth of an astral demon that opposes the ego as an enemy, wishing to alienate our astral body from the ego. Through its connection to the physical body, the astral body is anyway self-addicted. We can also say that the astral body is the craving and desire body that stands in opposition to the ego. There are beings, in particular Luciferic ones,[9] which love to make use of this egotistical desire element of our being and wish to alienate our ego. As we learn from inner schooling, a desire is only imbued with ego if we desire something that is in harmony with the world, with inner and outer life, and that does not lead a parasitic life of its own in a no-man's land of desire, estranged from reality—in Lucifer's realm.

Think about the visions of horror, of science fiction, that nowadays rear their heads everywhere in the media, and how much these already lead an independent life within people's souls. Everyone knows they have no reality but even so they still exert a sort of tension. Afterwards when the high has worn off, the soul feels hollowed out and waits for the next high, the next fascinating content.

There is no 'nothing' in this world—there are only beings with differing ways of working. When we fill ourselves with selfish and unrealisable wishes and desires, we bind ourselves to Luciferic beings who want to rob us of our power of ego, who want to take from us the control of our astral bodies and slide themselves into our ego by penetrating it as our 'lower ego'. Our present civilisation nurtures this and our constitution allows itself to be formed by it.

But when the ego has gone through the alienation process in the physical, the etheric and the astral, then it experiences how it is finally alienated from itself. This self-alienation can be recognised in our present loss of human identity, which is alienation at the level of the ego. Everywhere today, people speak of needing to affirm their identity anew, to seek for it anew. In this we can recognise the *mission* of evil: to wake us up to the right paths of development—but not to fall prey to evil itself!

Thus this fourfold alienation is not only there to threaten and endanger the ego, but it actually helps the ego wake up to the task that can be expressed as follows: I must seek my identity anew out of my own strength, by overcoming tendencies to alienation, and coming to myself. Then the experience of alienation is found to be one which awakens the consciousness of freedom in us through allowing us to encounter our potential for deviation.

Out of this consciousness of freedom, therefore, I would like to present an essential motif of inner schooling as a therapy to overcome this fourfold alienation.

In various places in his book of schooling, *How To Know Higher Worlds*,[10] Rudolf Steiner gives the conditions, the general rules which one has to follow throughout the whole path of schooling. These are valid as much for the continuous inner work of the initiate as for the beginner on the path of knowledge. These conditions link all human beings who are truly pursuing a spiritual schooling.

These 'accompanying' exercises have precisely the quality of helping to systematically secure the ego, actually in each of the members of the human being, and through this to give the ego strength and certainty on its path. Independently of all the special exercises or meditations done, the work on these conditions is at the same time a freeing of the self to its own true being, its own higher self, so that it can increasingly reveal itself as a source of strength throughout the whole human being, and actively connect itself to the world.

What Rudolf Steiner describes in the chapter 'Requirements for Esoteric Training' characterises the systematic path through all the members of the human being, culminating in a strengthening of the ego.

The physical body becomes the instrument of the ego if a person observes the requirement of taking care of their bodily and spiritual health. Can this lead to egotism, to an exclusive focus on one's own health? One might think: I must therefore look after myself, I must take care of myself both bodily and in soul ... However, what is described is how we have to learn to find the right relationship to pleasure—and to duty. Body and soul are harnessed in daily work, and it does happen that often one's health has to be neglected for the sake of duty. Perhaps one goes without a meal, or has to work through part or all of the night so that things can proceed. This means that work often requires us to neglect our health. What can have an unhealthy effect needs then to be balanced by the right relationship to pleasure. This means we should learn to enjoy things intensely, but in such a way that this enjoyment gives us the strength to sustain ourselves better in our work; that we learn never to seek out pleasure as an end in itself—which would then cost strength—but rather, learn to enjoy things in such a way that they give us strength and new motivation for duty.

Daily alertness in the forming of outer circumstances is one exercise. Of course, we must work on organising outer circumstances as healthily as possible and make clear to ourselves that enjoyment is allowed! Rudolf Steiner even makes it a condition! For its own health, the soul needs to be able to take pleasure. Joy and pleasure belong to the carrying forces in life. The problem is only one of arranging enjoyment in such a way that we stop at the point we should also stop at in eating: when it still tastes the best. For stopping at the height of enjoyment maintains our capacity to carry out our daily duties afterwards. If we go beyond the high-point, then in the case of food, we are so full that we become heavy and can no longer work properly.

This first condition is therefore actually a 'zenith-exercise': not missing the peak of the enjoyment; but then — taking the leap into work. We should relearn the art of pleasure, and not take a moralistic, denigrating stance towards it.

We see that this is an exercise, a lifelong task at which one can and must work. It leads, however, even if we take only a little trouble really consistently in this direction, to a new connection of the ego with the physical body and the outer circumstances of life.

A completely different world is the consolidation of the ego in the etheric body, the penetration of the ether-organisation by the ego — in the form of the second requirement. Here we are allowed to learn to experience ourselves as members of the whole. It is beneficial to work through all that can be experienced in the soul as obstacles preventing us from feeling ourselves part of a wider whole. Rudolf Steiner gives the example here of a cheeky pupil. If such a pupil behaves badly the whole day, then I can realize that this does not only have to do with this child — I am a part of it too, a part of the whole; it also has something to do with me. Is the child perhaps so impossible today because I gave a dull, routine lesson yesterday? Has he become like this during the night in order that this morning he can really offer me the chance to wake up and make more effort? How do I meet this child? Why has the inner contact broken off? Does he need to behave in such a conspicuous way so that I engage myself with him again?

The task is to enter for once quite selflessly into everything that surrounds me and to look at it as if it were a piece of myself, as if it had something to say to me, something to do with me. The etheric body is not just the sum of our life and thought forces, but it is also our social body; it is the organisation that makes us capable of connections and relationships.

The third requirement has to do with the astral body, where the ego has to consolidate itself. The exercise is to work systematically on the knowledge that thinking, feeling and willing are just as much realities as outer deeds. Every feeling is a being that emanates from me and touches and influences, either unpleasantly or positively, the person to whom it is directed. Every thought that I think about something, about a person, is a delicate etheric touch, a furtherance or a diminution of the sense of life of the other. Thoughts, feelings, desires, will impulses are soul-spirit realities for which we carry responsibility. 'Consolidation of the ego in the astral' means to take on the responsibility for what goes on in the astral body, and when an emotion arises to ask oneself: Will I leave it like that or should I transform it?

The next stage is to do with the consolidation of the ego in itself. The ego is very sensitive to recognition or disregard. It is still so embryonic, so much in development, that it is as sensitive as a young plant. Through the fourth requirement, we should now learn to make our identity ever more independent of outer recognition. This seedling 'ego' should, in a manner of speaking, gain protection and strengthening wholly from within—so that it can better resist heat and cold and also withstand a dry period. The meaning of my own ego development lies within, lies in the meaning that I give to myself and my deeds, and is not dependent on the meaning and importance that other people allot to them and by which they judge me. Gaining independence of outer judgement is a difficult exercise, as of course we rely on the acceptance or non-acceptance of our surroundings, and often need it so as to integrate our deeds into a situation in the right way. However, we must not become dependent on this.

The fifth to seventh requirements reach far beyond the ego into seed states of humanity's future development. Through tending the qualities mentioned there, the ego learns to anchor itself in its Spirit Self, in the beginnings of its Life Spirit, and even to have intimations of itself as Spirit Man. It also learns to use all these conditions in life. It becomes clear that the ego should be armed for its earthly task, for daily life. Therefore, at the end of the chapter, it is pointed out that life should be approached in such a way that these conditions are found in life itself, and through life find their affirmation. This means that we should work on these requirements in the midst of life, and not suppose that we would need solitude in order to become better human beings.

The question of the path of development, of schooling as a therapeutic task is, at the same time, the question of the opening up of the power of the ego through schooling. For in the end there is only one source of redemption, as much for ourselves as for the people who need help, and that is the sun power of the ego with its light and its warmth and its love. This we can bring into flow through this personal work on ourselves and it can then become an unconquerable source of strength in daily life.

2
The Path of Development as a Therapeutic Task for the Community in Professional and Daily Life

In pre-Christian times all the professions that had social significance, such as law, state administration, teaching, research, medicine, art, as well as building and architecture, were Mystery professions. The people who practised these professions received teaching and indications from the temple priests and initiates. The only remains of this in the public life of present times, albeit in a changed form, is the profession of the priest. Here alone a direct, horizontal succession is cultivated that reaches back to early Christian times and directly links up with the stream of grace which began to flow from the spiritual world through the Christ. This stream continued on through the apostles into humanity, and through the Service or Mass was further passed on from hand to hand, from head to head, from person to person—a horizontal stream of spiritual inheritance and impulse.

That is the only form which has visibly maintained itself in public life. In addition to this, there are the hidden esoteric communities in which—nowadays mainly as tradition only and not on the basis of their own spiritual revelations—a horizontal succession of the old spiritual traditions continues to be cultivated. These, however, do not lead to the practice of a particular profession in the public eye. Rather, all non-church professions of social importance have become secularised. As a result, it has more or less become impossible, for the present, for these professions to work in a really health-giving, socially constructive way.

For what does one need in order to work in a health-giving, socially constructive way? One needs the ability to look away from oneself, to look to the well-being of the other, to adjust oneself to the need for healing of the other person. This capacity for selfless service and help falls ever more into a twilight realm and is subject to severe criticism.

If, for example, we are in a group of nurses discussing the new professional identity of the nursing profession, we may hear expressed, almost as a cynical term of abuse, something that used to be the highest virtue: 'being on call twenty-four hours a day' — for the needs of the patients, for directions from the doctors. The nurses oppose this by saying such things as: 'We defend ourselves against this demanding attitude! We are also human beings, we also need something for ourselves, we cannot always "be on call" — what sort of expectations are those!' In this way the nurses are thinking through anew the tasks which their profession involves, right down to its very foundations.

An antipathy towards selfless serving is present — one easy to understand, because if such selflessness is demanded as a moral imperative, then it does not really come from within, it is not founded upon an individual's free will. In that case, it is not true and therefore neither stimulating nor strengthening for professional life. Indeed, it can even turn into its opposite and, instead of being satisfying, lead to exhaustion. Therefore it is understandable that for the time being one distances oneself from these old professional traditions which still derive from the Mysteries and which can now, finally, only maintain themselves within the church. It is also understandable that people say: We must seek for new professional values now and we must seek for them in such a way that our own development, our own future, our own ego can be fully involved. It is no longer possible to shut out personal development and at the same time forgo any personal existence. There is a clear consciousness of the fact that one's personal existence must be connected with one's spiritual existence, with one's professional existence, with ideal values. At the same time this marks the turning point between old and new Mysteries. In the old Mysteries the individual ego was not taken into account when higher teachings were received—on the contrary, it was excluded. As a result, selfless service to a higher task was easier to bring about than in a time like today when a Mystery knowledge or path of initiation is necessary which takes the ego into account and includes it. Therefore today we stand at the very beginning of a completely new cultural development. At the same time, the moment of initiation of humanity has arrived in the literal sense of the word. Initiation means beginning. The human ego itself determines the beginning of its new path of development for which it is itself responsible. The time of its minority has passed.

The problem which faces the caring professions today now becomes clear: in order to work therapeutically, we need qualities that are *truly therapeutic*. These can no longer be of an egoistical nature. That is a contradiction in itself. For another person is only healed by receiving what he needs for his healing. In order to recognise this, we must, as therapists turn away completely from our own need of healing, which may be of a quite different kind, so as to avoid the danger of projecting our own needs upon the other. The Mystery character of these professions must be found and worked on again in a new way if the work is to be healthy for both the helpers and those in need.

Rudolf Steiner was well aware of the difficulties connected with this when he gave the starting points for such new, professional, esoteric working. Despite this, it was still possible for him to indicate the direction to us, in the sense of a Christian Mystery founded upon the 'I am'. In the 'Curative Education Course',[1] in the twelfth lecture, he clearly spoke about how the path of development which one begins quite freely and personally, is at the same time the precondition for the path of schooling for professional work. If the personal ego is to be taken into account on the path towards receiving higher insight and revelation, then it must make itself capable of enduring it, through schooling. Indeed, it must go further and learn to love the revelations of the spirit! But this is only possible when self-love is so transformed that it becomes one with love for other people and for the world.

I will now try to sketch the basic elements of the path of schooling as given by Rudolf Steiner for the curative educationalists, and in so doing try to show that this path of schooling presupposes a *personal* willingness for one's own schooling.

Goethe's fairy tale *The Green Snake and the Beautiful Lily* shows how the river, which separates the sense-perceptible from the spiritual world, may be crossed by quite particular bridges. We can also recognise as a central motif the fact that this kind of bridge must be built anew. What are the building blocks of this bridge? What sort of bridge-building force is it that always connects the sense and spiritual worlds — regardless of the stage of consciousness of the initiate, regardless of whether the forces of knowledge can penetrate to the far side of this stream? Goethe's fairy tale answers this: it is only the fourth power
which is able to do that. After wisdom, beauty and strength, which rule on earth, it is the power of love that can erect this bridge. 'Love does not rule, but it creates and that is more', as the old man with the lamp tells the youth. This particular power is *the* central, strongest human power there is. Novalis, who was similarly initiated into the secrets of the threshold and its crossing — i.e. the secrets of the building of this bridge — expressed it in his *Hymns to the Night* as follows: '...but what became holy by the touch of Love, runs free through hidden ways to the region beyond...[2] Everything that we do with real love is directly perceived in the spiritual world. It reaches over. And that is the consolation, at the same time the rock upon which we can

build everything, and thanks to which we are always able to remain undaunted, because we can tell ourselves: Even if we know little, can do little, are often helpless and feel inadequate, love still remains to us the great field of work and practice. But it is also true that even if we *did* know everything, this knowledge must not make us so arrogant that it withers love within us. For then the entrance to the higher realms of the spiritual world would be closed. Pride in one's knowledge and the need for recognition are both inimical to an esoteric professionalism built upon love.

It was not for the curative educationalists alone, in the 'Curative Education Course', that Rudolf Steiner portrayed these two arch-enemies of the caring professions; he also made them visible to the Waldorf teachers in Stuttgart. There is a nice anecdote about this, which I would like to relate here as it was told to me: One day, when Rudolf Steiner returned to the Stuttgart Waldorf School, he went up the steps to the teachers' room. On the way he greeted a colleague and said: 'Down there in front of the school gates, two ladies are sitting. On no account must they enter the school.' He then went into the teachers' room. The colleague ran down quickly, wanting to see these two ladies. But when he reached the school gates, he saw no one. He was a little confused and asked someone else: 'Weren't there two ladies sitting here?' He was told no. He went back upstairs quite confidently and said: 'Herr Doktor, there are no ladies sitting down there.' Rudolf Steiner answered quite kindly: 'Yes there are! Two ladies have sat there for as long as I have known this school. But they must not come in. These two ladies are *Vanity* and *Desire for Recognition.*'

These are our two main enemies. A third important enemy to love-imbued work is the 'world-weary everyday person' ('marode Alltagsmensch'). In the pedagogical lectures and in personal conversations with the teachers of the Waldorf School too, Rudolf Steiner mentions this person.[3] The teacher, before going in to the children, is meant to hang himself up outside the classroom together with his coat. It is the same person that the priest covers up when he puts on his robes, to make clear: My mundane personal self, with its daily moods — which are justified in personal terms, but which are irrelevant for my profession — is covered up and transformed into a bearer of a professional and social responsibility, a higher jurisdiction. Because I belong to a profession, I take on the shared destiny of a large community of the same profession. A new, professional identity is obtained in addition to my personal one. It is something social, as I share the profession with others. For this I put on new clothing.

That has been maintained today among nurses, carers and doctors, even if some nowadays do not wear their white coats. It is not just hygienic reasons that make it sensible to wear a nurse's uniform — it becomes just as unhygienic in the course of work as ordinary dress does — rather, it makes visible the fact that I am on duty. One is also a little protected by these duty clothes. The personal human being no longer plays the same role. It steps back. Only when the uniform is taken off again is one back to being an ordinary, everyday person.

This uniform is something that we can put on consciously every day, even if we no longer have an outer uniform. It is, in truth, to do with having a spiritual mantle. This conscious putting on of a uniform as a manifestation of the particular soul-spirit attributes which we need for our profession, is the most important condition for the professional on the path of esoteric schooling. With which attributes must I clothe myself spiritually, if I want to practise my profession in a really helpful and useful way? This is the starting question of any inner schooling connected to a profession.

Rudolf Steiner gives the doctors a motto for their medical path and something of it appertains, of course, to all the healing professions. This motto is: *Having the will to do good.*[4]

If we remind ourselves of the passage in the New Testament, where the rich youth comes to Christ and says: 'Good Master...' and Christ repudiates this, saying: 'Why do ye call me good? No one is good except one: God'[5] then we can have some idea of what is meant by this force of goodness, and also what this goodness has to do with therapy: this will for good leads us into the region of the Father God. Here is the all-encompassing origin of being, from which the Son and Spirit Principles arise. In this all-encompassing Father Sphere, illness and its meaning belong as well.

In the 'Pastoral Medical Course', Rudolf Steiner describes the culmination of the paths of the doctor and the priest and, at the end, brings them together in the Pastoral Medical mantrum.[6] There we are told that it is the Father God Himself who sends illness to balance out karma.

Just as the Father sends the Son for the fulfilment of humanity's destiny, so he also sends illness to balance out karma. Therefore, if we want to heal, we must — at least in our feelings and attitude — place ourselves back into that time, into that consciousness which encompassed all humanity and allowed in evil, allowed in illness, but which also made individual destiny possible, whereby evil can be transformed again through free human deeds, through deeds of love, and illness can be healed.

We must link in to this Father-sphere with our goodwill and try to live in the mood: 'Not my will but Thy Will be done Father, for You know what is good for humanity, for the balance of karma.' It is then not surprising that in the 'Curative Education Course' Rudolf Steiner relates the central meditation specifically for the curative education profession to the Father God, and adds that one could also use the term 'God's Spirit' or something similar, as he wishes to invoke the primal 'All-Father' principle here, which encompasses and includes everything.[7]

The professional esotericism of the curative educationalist lives in this mood and also in that of therapeutic doing in general. This mood of being within the stream of purpose of the Father God's mission, of being destiny's companion with the task of healing, and balancing, is the robe that we may put on in spirit: the love for willing the good, the love for the Father God. From this love our love for our profession, for sick or handicapped people can be carried. This love carries us across the stream. It can build the bridge, the connection, and give the basis for the ensuing, more specific, exercises.

These are listed for us in the Curative Education Course and they lead to the development of those faculties which we need especially in curative education and social therapy. The first faculty is that of *flexibility:* always being aware that something quite new, a completely different attitude to what we thought, may be demanded of us. We must be flexible on all sides — open, perceiving, sensing, reacting, seeking, awake, alert, elastic in our soul.

This soul elasticity is, as it were, the overall virtue we need: at one moment one is putting out chairs in rows, in the next, sitting collectedly in the Service, doing justice to the most differing social situations and finding joy in the fact that things do not always go as planned — that is the exercise. Instead of pouring out a swarm of reproaches and apportioning blame to one's surroundings for what should have been thought and done in order that the present difficulty might have been avoided, we should ask: How do I rise to this unexpected situation? Flexibility is the magic word! With this virtue, we gain a tremendous economy of strength: a delicate smile appears on the face, flexibility is practised and at once the situation is directed along new, useful lines.

The fact that we grin at such a description indicates the second virtue, which directly belongs to flexibility: *humour*. Rudolf Steiner devotes some important words to this as well in the Curative Education Course. Humour is the little sister of love. There is no love without humour, even if humour cannot quite replace love. This little sister must always also accompany us in professional life.

Besides these two modern, unconventional virtues of flexibility and humour (Plato had not yet named them), we have a further three classical virtues. Through these we feel straight away the certainty of a familiar moral corset which we are acquainted with from earlier times. However, this must now be newly grasped and consciously worn. At the forefront of them is courage. For we need courage since we never know whether what we do with the best will in the world, and with flexibility, is actually what is right. On the one hand we need courage to do anything at all, and, on the other, we need it in order to bear our possible mistakes. Whoever can bear their mistakes can also dare to do great things because they are willing to carry on working, or to correct what was done wrongly through ignorance or inability.

It all has to do with the 'Courage to Heal'[8] that Rudolf Steiner emphasises as a central task of doctors for a real 'crossing of the threshold' — i.e. the readiness to do everything to the best of one's knowledge and conscience, without any guarantee of success, to be completely *with* the ill person: this kind of courage is also the central quality of will for the curative educationalist. Then comes the quality of attitude, of mood, the 'reverence for the small things'. Actually, it says in our course 'for the *very* smallest'.

What kind of quality is this reverence? It is the basic prerequisite for a meditative life. Reverence guides the consciousness-soul towards experiencing spiritual reality. The consciousness-soul develops itself by waking up through the physical plane, through the small things of the senses, the everyday things, the realities of life. If one manages to see these smallest, most physical, most external things in the light of the spirit, then the consciousness-soul leads the ego to awaken in the spirit. This means that if one can, through inner work, give meaning even to the smallest things, the greater connection lights up in one's consciousness, in which the smallest also has its place and meaning.

The third quality can be strongly experienced between head and heart, but it needs our whole understanding: it is *responsibility*, or also conscientiousness. This quality of being there conscientiously, responsibly for those being cared for, for the specific situation and circumstance; of creating a conscience by identifying oneself with things rather than by saying: 'That's not my problem!', to feel co-responsibility—this is the third 'classical' virtue of the curative educationalist.

Flexibility, humour, courage, reverence, responsibility — our soul-spirit uniform as it were—is woven from these five professional characteristics. However, when suitably clothed in this way, the question then arises: But now, what is the central exercise for the work itself, when we enter into it thus clothed?

Here we come to the central, pedagogical law. We should work in accordance with this law. The consideration of it, the observance of it, is at one and the same time the core of our professional, esoteric strivings. It is the central therapeutic principle, destiny-balancing and therefore healing. I would now like to describe this principle in respect to self-education—i.e. for one's own being.

What we experience in our ego has a direct effect on our astral body, with whose help, after all, we are able to experience the world and ourselves through thinking, feeling and willing. If we are happy, then this astral body is likewise moved, and strengthens itself; if we are sad, then it contracts, and can even be as if lamed or frozen.

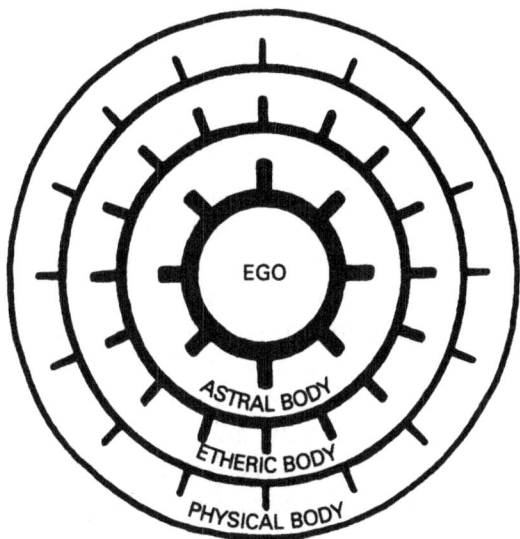

Interest in the world and interest in human beings are the two central characteristics of the ego through which it unites itself with the world and human beings. Thus the results of Rudolf Steiner's research, that the formation of a healthy body is the consequence of interest in the world, and of a healthy soul, the consequence of interest in other people, can well be understood. We can therefore see how our ego, with its interests, in the end determines health and illness in the widest sense.

Let us imagine that in this ego sphere (see diagram) we have a characteristic disinterest in the world and in people. The astral body similarly draws back, stiffens, becomes indifferent and ceases its sympathetic and thinking alertness. This, of course, has its effects on the etheric organism which is insufficiently stimulated and engaged by the astral body in regard to certain functions. The necessary vigour for its life-regulating activities is missing. Where interest is lacking, there is also nothing for the various members of the human being to do; and, as the human being is fundamentally intended to be an all-encompassing being, philanthropic and open to the world, there are many possibilities for failure, so that particular regions of one's own being become insufficiently cared for.

What now remains behind as a weakness in the etheric body, impresses itself—if it has happened over a long period of time—into the physical body and appears there as illness. In this manner, lack of interest can lead to constrictions in the soul realm, so that soul-spirit afflictions which are not overcome and worked through can impress themselves slowly into the physical-etheric constitution in the course of one life, already, and after 10, 20 or 30 years, become physical illnesses. Indeed, Rudolf Steiner describes how proper Waldorf pedagogy prevents children becoming ill so easily later on, as they have comprehensive interests and have learnt how to work things through in their soul. Looked at in this light, Waldorf pedagogy is unalloyed prophylaxis or illness-prevention for later life. This dimension is added to in the Curative Education Course by Steiner's descriptions of the fact that ego activity does not work only on the configuration of the astral body in the person themselves, but also directly influence the astral body of pupils; similarly the other members work on the next lower ones of the pupil. So curative educationalists must become aware to what a high degree all that they do can affect the health of their charges.

A second dimension of this principle is to be found in the lectures: *The Theosophy of the Rosicrucians.*[9] Here Rudolf Steiner describes how this principle is not only valid for one earthly life, but how, in accordance with it, the consequences of one earth life are visited upon the health of the next incarnation. The interests that lived in the ego in one life become the pre-condition for the particular constitution of the astral body in the following life on earth. This means that when I notice particular problems in my soul, in thinking, feeling and willing, I can then ask myself: How must my ego have been in the last life to have contributed to this astral body? I meet the karma of my last incarnation in my present soul body, in my soul's basic attitude and mood. And again, if I look at the conditions of life, my weakness or strength of resistance, my vitality, my sleep needs, my digestive capacities etc., then I have here and now a faithful image of my previous life on earth. In this way, I can know far more about this previous life than I would perhaps like to know...

We carry, as a dowry in the etheric body, what was not overcome in the soul in our last life, and needs to be worked on further. And what could not be worked through in the etheric body is now carried in us as visible illness in the physical body.

However, it goes even further. What we have done in the physical body in one earth life—suffered, experienced, what has been real, actual destiny, so to speak, as a physical person in a physical world, comes back towards us from outside as destiny in the following life on earth. I can draw conclusions about how my physical stance and behaviour was in the world in my last life, from the destiny that comes towards me now. Whatever arose through my physical body and went out into the world in my fourth life, comes back to me in my fifth life as destiny's answer. So we can see that illness and karma are most intimately connected. The Father God sends illness to balance karma, because when we begin to suffer etherically and physically in layers of soul that are increasingly less conscious, this suffering brings about the beginning of our healing, our overcoming of illness. When we learn to take up consciously into our destiny what ails us, we can say: This destiny-affliction that I am suffering is illness that was left over and not overcome in my previous earthly life. Whoever learns to consciously transform what has been left untransformed from a previous life, is also able to make working at their own destiny into a source of health for the other people whose destiny they are linked with, as is shown for the second condition (see diagram). This pedagogical law is the central law for self-education on all levels. The purification of the astral body takes place to the extent that we work on our thinking, feeling and willing; to the extent that we try to counter tendencies towards illness by nurturing the etheric, a clearing and clarifying of the etheric organisation arises. This is also true for the other realms.

As the last realm we experience karma itself which surrounds us as a social sphere, and affects us inwardly and outwardly as our human and world conditions. Whether the world is interested in us, whether people are interested in us, is in fact a karmic consequence of our own stream of interest in the last four incarnations. It is not chance whether we experience openness or reserve. Understood correctly, there are stages of awakening to ourselves, according to which we examine in the ego our capacity for interest; observe the degree of flexibility of our soul — how able it is to take things in, how ready to assimilate; then observe the etheric body — how much it carries us, how ordered it is, how supportive, how harmonious; then the physical body in its daily work; and finally, our circle of destiny in the social realm.

These are the sheaths of the ego and they are held together by this holy cloak of destiny that accompanies us through the incarnations. Rudolf Steiner has told us that it is the Christ Himself who has become the Lord of all our destinies. In the German language this is portrayed in the word ICH (I or ego) where the initial letters of the Christ are drawn together: Iesus CHristus. The Being of the Ego has become Lord of Karma since the Mystery of Golgatha. Now that the great Ego of humanity has united Himself with every single human ego, each human being with the help of Christ can become lord of their own destiny. Every single person, insofar as he acknowledges himself as an ego, is now consciously sheltered in this destiny of humanity. Therefore each is capable, not only of forming his own destiny, but also, consciously, that of humanity and of taking on co-responsibility. One can, through personal and social schooling, take hold of and order karma, and identify oneself more and more with the experience that it belongs to one's own being.

Knowing this is the most important basis of all pedagogical working. For if we cannot bring *ourselves* into order, how then should we wish to teach others to do so? It would be a contradiction in itself. If we do not wish to do this ourselves, then we have let our profession down.

Thus we have three levels of the effects of this great pedagogical law, with all the corresponding consequences for self-education. The lowest level of effect has to do with ourselves in regard to our constitution. The following level has to do with our karmic connections. The next, however, has to do with the mysterious, magical working between teacher and pupil, but also the magical working between all of us as colleagues in an institution. This pedagogical law is not only valid for the teacher and pupil. Just as it holds good for myself throughout one whole life, just as it holds good through the course of incarnations, so it also holds good in the minutest detail of personal contact between people. We can experience this in the simplest examples. Someone does not greet us—an outer expression of disinterest, an ego problem. Where do we experience it? In our soul. Immediately this disinterest affects our astral body. If this effect remains unchanged and consolidates, if the person really dislikes me and therefore does not greet me, and if I notice that and suffer from it; and if all of this takes place over years—if I do not learn to assimilate it— eventually it begins to work on the habit life of my etheric body and one day I become ill. There are many people who say that this or that person makes them ill; the process can be described exactly. Therefore it is according to this pedagogical law that an encompassing human love can be brought about—but it is also the principle through which individual and social health can either be cultivated or harmed.

Even if I have a justified anger or a deep antipathy towards someone, I must still ask myself, in accordance with the virtues of responsibility and conscientiousness that I need to acquire: Do I really want to harm that person because of this? 'Love your enemies, do good to them which hate you.'[10] The words of the Gospel may at first appear to us as a constricting moral postulate or as the opposite of a 'normal' soul reaction. However these words are, if taken literally, the teaching of the most elementary, most selfless human love, the source of healing compassion. For the therapist this is particularly pertinent. A doctor operates on friend or foe equally carefully. In principle there is no difference.

We can also see though, how at times it can be necessary to strictly separate personal and professional life; to say to oneself: Professionally, I will and can do this or that; but for my personal life I must nonetheless keep away from certain things because I am unable to cope with them. Another virtue comes in here, one that is not specific to a profession, but rather a general esoteric one, valid in all schooling, by which all esotericism stands or falls: honesty. This must be grounded, though, in honesty about oneself. Many things occur, including feeling powerless, because we demand things of ourselves that, in all honesty, we either do not really want to do or are incapable of doing—yet we still do them. Many social problems also derive from the fact that we expect something of others that they cannot give or be. Only honest, realistic evaluation of oneself and the world will help here, and the striving to make the best of what is available.

This pedagogical law, also called the chief law by Rudolf Steiner, underpins our personal and professional life. Self-education fructifies education; education works back positively on to self-education, and spurs it on. Through this law the secret of Goethe's fairy tale is also revealed. For it describes how two things are to be united with each other in order to build the bridge to the spiritual world in every moment of the day. The power of the depths of the will, the good will—embodied in the snake—sacrifices itself to the light of knowledge, the light of the spirit, through which this snake can become transparent like a precious stone. Earthly will thus becomes illumined and carried by the spirit and can therefore work in a healing, bridge-building way—also between people.

3
The Path of Development as a Therapeutic Task for the Connection of the Individual with Humanity

The question of schooling for ourselves and for our professional activity always has a two-sided aspect: one of knowledge and the other of will.

We transform ourselves and the world by educating ourselves in accordance with our knowledge. But the actual transformative element is our will, our activity. This is also true of the area that we are going to consider now: the *dimension of all humanity* in the path of schooling. This, too, has its knowledge and its transformation aspect. In this century, for the first time in the history of the world, interest in the whole of humanity has become a fact for countless people. In earlier centuries, even in the time of the great discoveries and colonisations, only specific parts of the world were in people's consciousness. Only in the twentieth century has it become possible—through the world wars on one hand but also through the invention of radio, television, telephone and fax on the other—for each individual person to develop a global consciousness quite independent of where they are on the earth's surface.

This globalisation speaks directly to the leanings of the younger generations, particularly those from the middle of the century on. Young people—one can see this nowadays in every school—suffer too when some event takes place somewhere else in the world. They are affected too. I can still remember from my own school days—and it was the same for others—that during the Vietnam War there were days when I had no appetite because of the nerve gas attacks there which were making the leaves fall from the trees. It was a terrible thought; Vietnam was somehow as close for us as the next town. In the streets of my own town there were demonstrations against the Vietnam war. This is the literal, present-day meaning of 'common sense' — and such common consciousness is a wonderful characteristic of modern people.

A second kind of global quality to do with humanity, that lives in every young person today, is a fine sense of social justice and injustice. Young people have a deep antipathy to authoritarian power structures and imperialistic attitudes. The so-called 'revolution of 68' was a first, clearly articulated example of this.

A third quality that we can observe is the urge for spiritual independence. Older people may wonder why younger ones are so hesitant to join the Anthroposophical Society, even though it would seem to be the most natural thing in the world ... but nowadays we want to do everything ourselves in our own way, not too early — and particularly not if someone else urges us to.

In all of this, something of an encompassing principle of tolerance is speaking. A spiritual independence is sought — for oneself and for others — to the point of reacting allergically if non-anthroposophical spiritual directions are, as a matter of course, regarded as questionable. One wants each person to have the right to their own spiritual search for a path, without any standardisation. A wholesale tolerance in religion and spirituality, a fine sense for social justice and a feeling of brotherhood with the whole of humanity, are emerging as needs.

Looking ahead, Rudolf Steiner had perceived these qualities and had also made clear the spiritual context in which they stand. He described how our higher ego rests in the lap of our angel, who weaves these three ideals as developmental possibilities into our astral body, in our unconscious depths of will. Brotherliness in connection with humanity, religious freedom for the soul, and the possibility of setting out on an individual, spiritual search, i.e. of reaching the spirit through thinking.

We see the efficacy of these unconscious imaginations, these unconscious will impulses, but we see their counter images too. For the danger these same young people run is—if they cannot bring these impulses into consciousness strongly enough—that the yearning for tolerance is perverted to indifference, to a total relativity, to a complete unconnectedness, where nothing of any meaning can take place and where no effort is worthwhile. As a result, many young people fall into a certain bitterness, as the conditions in which they live correspond so little to this ideal of tolerance. Everywhere they come up against the remnants of old power structures; they experience hate instead of brotherliness, and also the growth of fundamentalist tendencies whose very aim is to destroy individual freedom once again. A profound cultural antipathy, helplessness, even bitterness comes to burden the conscious part of the soul, and becomes noticeable as a hindrance in everyday life. It is like two sides of the same coin—the positive and the negative. We can feel quite acutely that negative aspects will gain the upper hand if a clear impulse does not arise to really enable the positive qualities to be raised into consciousness and used.

This new impulse, which in our times had to come so as to enable people to raise the forces for good, that live instinctively in the will, into the clear light of consciousness, has not, of course, appeared from nowhere.

I first wish to describe the Mystery background. Just as we could say the old Mysteries have come to an end and that a secularisation has taken place, so too we can say that a new Mystery path is urgently needed so that a clear orientation can illumine our chaotic and increasingly difficult times. But one thing is quite obvious: things cannot evolve in the same way as in the old Mysteries any more, in which single individuals stood out as the great leaders of humanity, for this individual realm is now present in each single human ego. Everyone is a potential king! Everyone is a potential ruler, everyone can become an initiate! No one wants to subject themselves to anyone else. The ego has become so strong and so individual through the effect of Christianity that a new culture can now only arise if single egos join together in full freedom, in the service of self-determined, spiritual goals.

The possibility must now arise, however, for such spiritual perspectives — which are healing for our times and which lead humanity further — to be found. The objection may be raised: Why do these perspectives need to be found? Isn't everything already there in the Christian Gospels? Of course, everything that can lead to a renewal of the Mysteries is contained in them, but a bottomless chasm yawns between the pictorial language of the Gospels and the materialistic thought habits of present day humanity. To begin with there is no bridge. This bridge must first be built. Materialistic thinking with its scientific orientation must find a connection to the revelations of Christianity and learn to take them up. To this end, these revelations must be formed and formulated in a way of thinking which can gain access to the consciousness of modern people. Goethe was able to illustrate this task in the poetic images of his fairy story, *The Green Snake and the Beautiful Lily*. Furthermore, help in this direction can be found in his scientific writings, particularly his *Theory of Colour*. But then he too reached a boundary. He could not describe the path of initiation itself, which is the keystone of the bridge to understanding the necessary theory of knowledge. He broke off his fragment, *The Mysteries* — it was not yet possible to proceed.

It was left to Rudolf Steiner, as an initiate in our epoch, to prepare himself to complete this work and bring the new impulse. He prepared himself by educating his thinking so that it was possible for him not only to penetrate spiritual vision with thinking, but also with 'materialistic' sense perception, which for us nowadays initially appears devoid of spirit. There have been many clairvoyant people in this century. What makes Rudolf Steiner different from them is his ability to leave his innate clairvoyance to one side. This meant an enormous amount of inner work for him, as he was already a born clairvoyant. For him as a child, the dead mingled with the living. He noticed very early on that there were things that other people did not see and about which he therefore could not speak because they would become alarmed; and that there were things about which he could speak because others could see them as well.

Then his whole childhood and youth were filled with the longing to very gradually unite these two states of consciousness, so that everyone, if they wanted to, could find this bridge themselves. Not until he reached mid-life did it first become possible for him, by bringing the greatest concentration to bear, to perceive a plant, a stone, a person in such a way that the spiritual aura, the spiritual reality disappeared for him, and only what other people usually see remained visible.

This was the pre-condition for his being able to write in his autobiography, *The Course of My Life*, of how he came to stand before the Mystery of Golgotha in a most earnest, most holy celebration of knowledge. Only after he himself had fully experienced the death of the spirit and had immersed himself solely in materialistic human consciousness, which is bound and chained to the sense world, could he experience the complete inner breakthrough to the resurrection from this grave of materialism and soul death, to the revelation of the Christ-Being and the Event of Golgotha. It was this experience alone which enabled him to become the great initiate of Christ, the great messenger of Christ for the present day, the messenger of the Representative of Man.

At the same time, however, he could also reveal the Mystery of Europe, the task of Europe for the world. For Europe was protected by invisible powers, so that in the post-Christian centuries following the turning point of time, an historical area could slowly be formed here, through the migrations of peoples, in which a Christianisation could take place. At first Christianity penetrated into this new Europe as pure will- and soul-content. Up to the Middle Ages this was only in pictures and words — in the form of chanting, cultic ritual, such as the Latin Mass, of which people understood nothing, yet still experienced the atmosphere, the mood. The truth of Christianity slowly penetrated into this soul- and will-life over the centuries.

In the Middle Ages, in the late Middle Ages, in all of Scholasticism, thinking slowly became capable of bringing its full strength to bear on these Christian truths, and of attempting to understand them. The awakening, modern capacity of thought was first schooled through the Christian Articles of Faith. Later it became increasingly oriented to sense perception alone. In the differentiation between Nominalism and Realism, two paths of thinking in European development began to define themselves: a small stream which maintained the spirituality, the search for the Christ in thinking, and a larger one, involving the greater part of humanity, that allowed the spirituality of thinking to fall to earth as it were, and wanted to use thinking only for the purpose of understanding external sense phenomena. Materialistic science began, step by inexorable step, to rule the human mind.

Europe is the place in which it became possible for human beings to develop an individual life of thought, of knowledge. Neither in the Orient and Asia, nor in the West in American culture, nor in the South in African culture does one find signs of an indigenous materialistic consciousness and the development of individual thought. This was a purely European event in the history of humanity. From Europe, a conquering stream flowed through the other continents and countries. Six months before the Christmas Foundation meeting, Rudolf Steiner tells us in the 'Imagination of Europe'[1] that helping to protect this European area from the spiritual influences of the East and the magical influences of the West, constituted a task for the spiritual world itself. For this delicate seedling of freedom of individual consciousness would have been immediately overcome and squashed by the spiritual-magical supremacy. It is a miracle that it was not until Goethe's time that the Orient began to exert more influence, so that an ancient wisdom entered the consciousness of European people.

In our century this time of protection has come to an end. Due to the world wars and the falling away of many boundaries, this European area is now open, and Oriental and Western spirituality have flooded into Europe with all the dangers that this brings for individual freedom. Now each single person stands before the task which also confronted Rudolf Steiner: to find the bridge from materialistic consciousness, to which we owe our freedom, across to spiritual consciousness, without losing the freedom we have attained and without annihilating again the purpose of European evolution.

Just as materialism streamed out from Europe over the whole world so that the impulse to freedom became a global one, so this same Europe, where everything streams together and mingles, now has the task of giving the individual the evolutionary possibility of forming thinking into a bridge again between the concrete, researchable, sense-perceptible world and the spiritual laws and worlds of being that can only be grasped in pure, clear thinking. Freeing thinking again from its imprisonment in the sense world by this individual deed, and bringing a spiritualising of thinking into the world, is the new impulse which leads into the future. That is the therapeutic task of the path of schooling for humanity that is given to us Europeans. And I would like to say at this point: anyone who understands this task is a European. This can be the case in any country in the world, if one knows how this bridge between the material and the spiritual can truly be constructed and crossed, in freedom. Certainly, the possibility of building this bridge originated in Europe, in Middle Europe, but now it can be built anywhere on the earth. Stimulating and realising this bridge-building—that is the spiritual task of Europe. Europe is the cultural area where the preconditions were achieved which enabled a person—Rudolf Steiner—to fulfil this task, to begin with on behalf of everyone else. Now that it has been achieved once, anyone can learn it. It is our task to understand this message and take it out into the whole world.

In the old Mysteries, spiritual beings descended to human beings and taught the initiates. The Mystery centres were visible temples on earth, and this descent and embodying of spiritual beings took place there. The new Christian Mysteries that reckon with the full freedom of the individual cannot, in the same way, be places of radiant, spiritual revelation on earth. That would be incompatible with individual freedom, for each person would stand in the thrall of this revelation and would have to accept it. One would be blinded, fascinated, and forget oneself. This would no longer be right for our times. That kind of Mystery culture is over and done with.

So what must a Mystery culture look like, which fulfils the same task as the old Mysteries, but now takes the freedom of individual people into account?[2] Decisive from now on is that the temples are to be sought in the supersensible world, as was already described in the Middle Ages in relation to the Grail Temple. If one reads the geographical indications of Wolfram von Eschenbach,[3] one discovers that this Grail Castle is not in the visible world, even if Grail Castles and Grail Churches have existed and still exist, built by human hands as reflections of these supersensible temples. Richard Wagner has Lohengrin say: 'In a distant country, unreachable by your steps, lies a castle called Monsalvasch.'

Through his schooling, Rudolf Steiner, the great Christ initiate, not only developed a dawning awareness, as Goethe did, of this supersensible temple of humanity, but fully perceived and entered into it. But in addition he also succeeded in making this temple visible for our thinking, for our feeling, for our willing.

But what happens to freedom in the new Mysteries now? They are not like the old Mysteries of Wisdom where pupil was dependent on teacher. Nowadays, the wisdom of the old Mysteries has to a large extent become general knowledge. Also anthroposophical spiritual science and the great wisdom of Eastern and Western cultures are accessible to anyone. Everyone has the possibility of being a teacher, and also of preserving their freedom while learning from others. Rudolf Steiner demanded of his pupils that they should not believe what he said but think it through, and thus learn to work with it independently. The new Mysteries are, in the sense of keeping 'new wisdom' secret, no longer Mysteries. They are Mysteries of the Will. We sleep in our will. We do not know what rests in the depths of our will, in our desires and inclinations. We know only about what suddenly awakes as need, as wish, as striving in actual life situations, in human meetings, in events of destiny. And then we feel ourselves free to suddenly will something. We think for ourselves about such things as: How can I do that? How can it be brought into connection with all that I have done earlier? And then we place our thinking at the service of these will impulses that have awakened. The awakening of the will is totally compatible with human freedom. Everything can be tested through individual, independent thinking, and felt with the feeling, before one follows one's will. It is called self-mastery when we do only what we really will to do, what we ourselves have recognised to be right.

The secret of this new Mystery is that, before birth, we ourselves were all in the temple in the spiritual world.

There we were Mystery pupils of the Epoch (Time) Spirit, Michael, and his hosts; we have met each other in the Michael School, in this spiritual temple, and have taken deeply into our most sacred will decisions about what we want to do for the goals of this temple of humanity, in the service of the Christ-Being on earth. This pre-birth decision, this pre-birth initiation of our will is, however, only present in our sleeping will. With the help of the ideas of anthroposophy which can grasp the spiritual world, it is now our task on earth to reach these will impulses, to waken this will; to raise the snake, to make it transparent, to shine through it with thinking, to illuminate it with the gold of wisdom and to come, in this working together of thinking and willing, to a community-forming capable of carrying the great tasks and goals of humanity in the present time.

Rudolf Steiner has paved the way for this creation and building of community in the Anthroposophical Society and the School of Spiritual Science. This community-forming was intended from the first to be such that free human spirits, independent of religion, race and nationality, independent of language or other adherences, could come together here from all over the world in order to reflect and bring to mind their task for humanity.

The Foundation Stone Meditation[4] is the spiritually connecting element upon which everything we do in the Anthroposophical Society is founded. It calls on the forces of the human soul as it lives in each single person throughout the world—in the head, in the heart, in the limbs—and orientates the human soul to the Christ Being as the central being of humanity. A Christ-seeking human community, whose task is focused upon humanity's knowledge and will, has been founded in the Anthroposophical Society.

The Anthroposophical Society is not only a community of shared ideas but also a community of humanity. It is formed from the individual members who join together in groups. In these self-chosen working groups, the members may all be quite similar to one another. But the representative of this group, the group leader, will be in fraternal contact with the representatives of other groups, which can already be working in a quite different way. Then these representatives and group leaders meet and name a regional representative who again meets with other regional or national representatives. Finally, these national representatives meet together and again represent the regional representatives. Thus the building of a human community reveals itself to us, in which is living each single soul of the community. As they all meet together in freedom of spirit, no one finds it necessary to make their representative role a vehicle for their own self-expression; instead they represent the people of the group and become the guardian of what lives within it. Such a person knows more or less what the members would say in a particular situation and endeavours to represent these impulses.

Finally, this social structure of the Anthroposophical Society comes to a conclusion in the circle of the Vorstand (or executive committee) at the Goetheanum. This circle confers with the national representatives on matters to do with the whole of humanity and strives to make a useful contribution in the service of humanity as a whole. It is important to work through what the people in the various countries can contribute, not just for the culture of their own country, but also for the health of the whole human community. This can only succeed if the work is orientated towards the goals of humanity and not to national trivialities. Therewith a magnificent social building task is given us.

Within this Society, Rudolf Steiner founded the School of Spiritual Science (Freie Hochschule für Geisteswissenschaften) at the Christmas Foundation Meeting. In doing so he drew the following diagram:[5]

Here you can see that he has written 'General Anthroposophical Society' in shorthand (Allg.Anthr.Ges.) on the blackboard. And then above it, 'establishing of the First Class of the School of Spiritual Science'; then above that, 'establishing of the Second Class'; and again, above that, 'establishing of the Third Class'. Through Rudolf Steiner's deed, this School is the supersensible Michael School now brought down into the realm of human thinking. It cannot enter the physical world because the Michael being can only descend to the etheric world, to the world of thought in human beings. But here, from below, out of the spiritual tradition of the Middle Ages and esoteric Christianity, the Rosicrucian School grows towards this Michael School and interpenetrates it in the etheric world, in the sphere of thought. Thus in the First Class, the Rosicrucian School coming from the earth and the Michael School coming from the spiritual world conjoin with each other. This gives each person the possibility of connecting themselves directly with the working and revelation of the spiritual world. In this picture by Rudolf Steiner, the Sections are drawn in a way that expresses the fact that they reach down and take hold from above downwards.

In *How To Know Higher Worlds*, the path to the temple of knowledge is described. In the Mystery Dramas[6] the path to the temple of love and destiny is described. In the School of Spiritual Science, in the First Class, is described the path to the realisation of the spiritual impulses that can be recognised and felt within the realities of daily life. This is the social temple, the temple of life, the temple which in Goethe's sense 'stands on the river', and where the bridge over the stream arches itself for all human beings to cross.

Rudolf Steiner has made us conscious of humanity's unconscious crossing of the threshold in our century. He has made conscious what sleeps in our will and has raised it up into daily life, into our daily thinking and doing, so that we are able to learn to consciously realise goals from the other side of the threshold, to realise spiritual impulses in the daily life of all professions.

I would like to close these thoughts with the words that Rudolf Steiner spoke again and again in the esoteric lessons, and which he finally wrote down in a special form in a notebook in Norway in the year 1921.

The words are directed to the great masters, to the great teachers of humanity in the past, the present and the future. These words encompass this attitude to humanity, this love for humanity and the inner will to build a humanity that can really carry and realise what is human. Rudolf Steiner first wrote this couplet:

'The world building must arise
Of human beings must it be built'[7]

Then comes:

Masters of Yore:
In shuddering awe
My spirit eye perceives
Your enlightened wisdom
To your realms let strive
My soul's purpose
To build on the human world-building with you.

Masters of the Present:
In willing devotion
May my ear hear
Your creating world-word
That the world goals
Are not eternally lost to human beings
Who must then fall prey to Lucifer.

Masters of the Future:
In love-filled willing
I join my own ego
To your world-willing.
Human force of will
Should unite itself with
Might-creating *world-word*

In love-filled willing
My own ego joins itself
With your world-willing;
Only in this may it hope
To find itself spared
From Ahriman's soul cold.[8]

Meister der Vorzeit:
In schaudernder Ehrfurcht
Erblickt mein Geistesauge
Eure lichte Weisheit
In Eure Regionen strebe
Mein Seelensinn
Mit Euch zu bauen an dem Menschen-Welten-Bau.

Meister der Gegenwart:
In williger Andacht
Erhöre mein Seelenohr
Euer schaffend Weltenwort
Dass nicht ewiglich verloren
Der Mensch dem Weltenziele
Und Lucifer verfallen müsse.

Meister der Zukunft:
Im lieberfüllten Wollen
Verbind ich Eigen-Ich
Mit Eurem Welten-Wollen
Es soll vereinen sich
Des Menschen Willenskraft
mit krafterzeugendem Weltenwort.

Im lieberfüllten Wollen
Verbinde sich das Eigen-Ich
Mit Eurem Weltenwollen
In ihm nur darf es hoffen
Von Ahrimans Seelenkälte
Verschont sich selbst zu finden.

Part Two

1
Medicine at the Threshold

To ordinary, not directly clairvoyant, consciousness the threshold to the spiritual world[1] reveals itself in a threefold way. It passes through every human heart. Here the inner world of thoughts, feelings and will impulses, the soul and spirit, meets together with that part of the external world and physical body which is brought into consciousness by the senses. This threshold, however, can also be experienced in every striving for knowledge, when we attempt to connect percept and concept—i.e. sensory and super-sensory facts—in a truthful way. We meet this threshold again with the coming and passing away of the human being through birth and death, with his appearance and disappearance in the visible realm of time.

In the field of medicine, too, this threefold threshold situation meets us daily—even if those concerned are hardly, or not at all aware of it.

What is the force that leads us to the threshold and allows us to cross it more or less consciously? It is our essential being itself, the core of the personality, our ego-nature. It is this ego whose independent activity connects percept and concept in an experience of truth. It is also this ego that makes true connections between one person and another, and makes known our own higher nature through the heart's voice of conscience. And it is the ego which clothes itself in its bodily sheaths[2] at the time of birth or releases itself from them in dying. Thus the experience of the threshold is amongst the most central ego-experiences of the human being, even if there are countless people who are not conscious of this fact as such. In earlier times this secret of the threshold was known only to a few, being reserved for the initiates in the Mystery Schools and Temple institutions alone. This was necessary, as a strict schooling and preparation were needed for consciously enduring and crossing the threshold. For at the threshold is revealed all that separates the human being from consciously grasping his true nature, his higher self. Every form of egotism — from the tiniest untruthfulness, through the most varied forms of lovelessness, to the will impulses whose sources and goals are insufficiently clear — separates us from the divine source of our true being and plunges us into the abyss that opens between the two worlds of the divine and the earthly, into which we are placed as evolving human beings.

Only in our century has the knowledge of the initiates from old and modern times become accessible to humanity.[3] But only in our century, as well, have human beings progressed so far in their development that they can fully experience the separation between the spiritual world and the sense world, resulting in the global spread of materialistic and technical culture. People no longer experience an instinctive certainty carrying them. Church faith is also questioned by ever-increasing numbers of people, more and more consciously and from a perspective of independence. Thus it has become a necessity of our times to acknowledge that we are standing at the abyss between the sense and spirit worlds, and to transform the unconscious experience of the threshold into an actively conscious one. This is particularly true for medicine, since it, as no other science, has daily involvement with all three aspects of the threshold in human existence; and can only use physical, soul and spirit remedies in a manner worthy of human beings by developing as great an insight into these realities as possible.

The Human Foundations of Science, Art and Religion

From time immemorial, human strivings in science, art and religion have enabled people to connect themselves with the spiritual world. These strivings formed the basis of culture and society. With the rise of Nominalism, which also allowed materialistic science to develop, natural science in particular separated itself from spiritual knowledge. The ideal arose of an objective science, independent of the human ego. Through this, art also lost the capacity to reveal direct spiritual vision or thought, becoming more and more of a leisure and holiday activity. Finally, religious life became, and is, a private affair and plays only a subordinate role in public life.

Once more uniting these three archetypally human cultural activities with real spiritual knowledge and experience, is one of the great tasks of anthroposophy. Thus in three successive phases in the development of the Anthroposophical Movement and Society, science, then art, and finally religion were renewed, the latter as an independent movement for religious renewal. This is however only one part of the great task. It is not just to do with renewing these three areas and uniting them again with real spiritual life, but above all involves recognizing how these three areas work together in a living way; and making this interaction the basis for new social forms. Rudolf Steiner says on 30 January 1923:

> So we may say that Anthroposophy begins in every case at the scientific level, calls art to the enlivening of its concepts, and ends in a religious deepening. It begins with what the head can grasp, takes on all the life and colour of which words are capable, and ends in warmth that suffuses and reassures the heart, so that man's soul can at all times feel itself in the spirit, its true home. We must learn, on the anthroposophical path, to start with

knowledge, then to lift ourselves to the level of artistry, and to end in the warmth of religious feeling.[4]

The threefold human being is the original source of the three spheres of scientific, artistic and religious activity: with the help of thinking we become scientists, with the help of feeling we learn to feel and create artistically, and with the help of willing we become capable of religious devotion.

In the 'French Course',[5] Rudolf Steiner describes the connection between the human sheaths and science, art and religion:

Physical body—modern science;
Etheric body—true philosophy that breaks through to living thinking;
Astral body—cosmology, the soul's self-recognition in its feeling of oneness with the universe;
Ego—religion, the devotion of being to being.

If we now look at the threefold human being and at how, in the nerve-sense system, in the rhythmic system and in the metabolic system respectively, the bodily sheaths work together with each other, then the following arises[6] (see diagram):

In the nerve-sense system—as indicated by Rudolf Steiner and Ita Wegman in the second chapter of *Extending Practical Medicine* (Fundamentals of Therapy)[7]—conditions are such that the ego organisation manifests in a soul-free form in thinking. We owe this to the fact that we are not only able to feel ourselves freed from the body and really 'at one' with what we are thinking about, but that we thereby also have the capacity to stand back from ourselves in spirit, to get distance from ourselves. We are able to make clear to ourselves the remarkable fact that in thinking we are—usually without realising, or knowing it—outside our bodies. This means that in thinking we cross the threshold

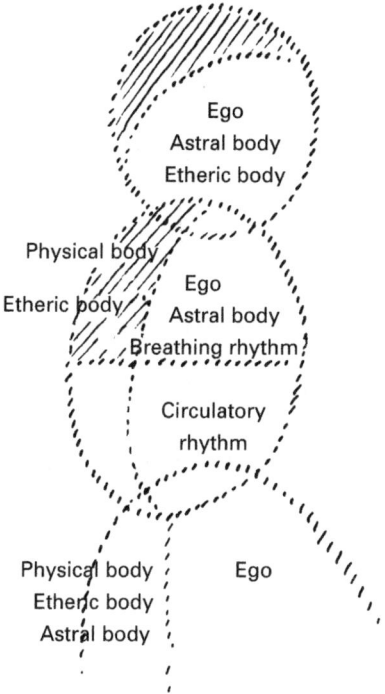

to the spiritual world, but usually unconsciously. If we look at our feeling life, we can see how our ego and astral body are also to a large extent active outside the body. The astral body penetrates more deeply into the bodily frame when we breathe in, and when we breathe out returns to the ego again, whose activity unfolds in feeling itself and being united with and immersed in the world. Here too, we have a partial leaving of the body, something we are also not conscious of in ordinary life. In the metabolism, in contrast, all four sheaths are closely connected with each other and completely incarnated in the body. Here a full crossing of the threshold is possible only at death.

If we now look at the connection of science, art and religion with the constituent levels of the human being, it becomes clear that an enlivening, a working together of scientific, artistic and religious possibilities can be reached in all three areas. Where the ego consciously awakens in thinking, the will also awakens in thinking, and spiritual communion can then arise, i.e. 'the perception of the idea within reality'.[8] But it becomes clear, as well, why the artistic endeavour that arises in the middle realm can lead directly to new knowledge on the one hand, and on the other into religious experience. Lastly, these basic facts of the human condition can lead us to see why the most sacred mystery of the Christian religion is contained in the Transubstantiation of the bread and the wine, the spiritualising of substance through the process of metabolism. Transubstantiation is the most archetypal and self-sufficient religious element of all. This can take place, however, at the level of body, soul or spirit. It can only take place though, when all four sheaths work together in the threefold human being under the guidance of the ego.

In our questions about standing at the threshold, it becomes clear why, today, so infinitely much depends not only on modern people becoming aware of the lack of a spiritual connection in their lives, but also on them recognizing that the activity of thinking is what can first assimilate real spiritual content, thereby giving the ego the possibility of living in the world of thought as if in a spiritual world. The ego can therefore cross the threshold consciously on the paths of thinking, and experience itself as the bridge over the abyss. Taking this life of thinking illuminated by the spirit as the starting point, the life of feeling and of will can then be inspired anew and stimulated to spiritually orientated, artistic and social deeds. This awakening in thinking to a new experience of the spirit has, however, a marked effect on human health.

From the Temple Sleep of the Egyptian Mysteries to the Hygienic Occultism of Today

In her foreword to Rudolf Steiner's lectures on 'Universe, Earth and Man', Marie Steiner[9] describes the situation of western esotericism as follows:

> The individual personality had to come into being, it had to comprehend itself, take itself in hand and recognize itself as a focal point, to confront and then overcome itself, to learn to die, that it might grasp hold of itself again as a free ego-being whose core is the divine ego.
>
> This is the path of western esotericism, which the European cannot avoid. Formerly his task was to thoroughly permeate and form the personality entangled in egotism; his present task is to overcome egotism, to transmute it into the free, strong ego-being which seeks the divine and is not driven by desires and instincts. He can only do this by mastering his forces of consciousness, through perceiving and knowing.[10]

In these lectures on 'Universe, Earth and Man', Rudolf Steiner describes the deeper connections between the ancient Egyptian cultural epoch and our present fifth Post-Atlantean one.[11] He first portrays the Egyptian practice of mummification, and its importance for the development of modern materialism. Then he speaks of the nature and task of the temple sleep, and its parallel in modern culture:

> Let us now, in a few brief strokes, sketch out a picture for our souls of the nature of the temple sleep, which was one of the remedies employed by the priests of Egypt. Anyone whose health had been in some way impaired was not treated with external medicines and remedies; there were only a few of these and they were seldom used. Sufferers were instead taken to the temple and there put into a kind of sleep. It was not an ordinary sleep but a

kind of somnambulistic state, which was intensified to such a degree that the patient became capable of having full-scale visions rather than just chaotic dreams. During this sleep the patient perceived etheric forms in the spiritual world, and the wise priests understood the art of influencing these etheric pictures which passed before the sleeper—they could control and guide them.

Let us suppose that an invalid was put into a temple-sleep. The priest, skilled in medicine, was at his side, and formed and fashioned the etheric visions in such a way that there actually appeared before the sleeper, as if by magic, those forms which at one time the ancient Atlanteans had looked on as their gods. These divine forms, of which the various peoples still possessed a memory in their mythologies—German, Norse and Greek—were now placed before the soul of the person who was in the temple sleep. He saw, in particular, certain figures and forms which were connected with the healing dynamics [...] The wise priest guided this dream life in such a way that powerful forces were released during the etheric visions, and these restored to order and harmony the forces of the body which had fallen into disorder and discord. [...]

This self-elevation to the spirit contained in ancient times a healing element; and it would be good for people to learn to understand this once more, for then they would understand the great misssion of the anthroposophical movement—which is to lead the human being back up to the worlds of spirit, so that he may again enter those worlds from which he has descended. It is true that in future people will not have induced in them a somnambulistic condition; conscious self-awareness will be fully preserved, yet strong forces of the spirit will nevertheless become active and effective within them, and the possession of wisdom and insight into higher worlds will then be capable of exerting a healing, harmonizing influence on human nature.

Today, this connection between the spirit and the art of healing is hidden, so that those not initiated into the deeper wisdom of the Mysteries can hardly perceive it. They are unable to discern the subtle realities that exist. But those who can look more deeply know upon what profound inner conditions healing can depend. Let us imagine, for instance, that someone falls prey to a certain illness, and that it has an inner cause — not something like a fractured thigh-bone or an upset stomach, which are also influenced by external factors.

Anyone wishing to explore this deeply will soon find that a person who enjoys occupying himself with mathematical ideas will have a quite different potential for being healed than will someone who who does not like concerning himself with mathematics. This fact demonstrates the remarkable connection between a person's inner mental life and the state of their outward health. [...]

Take another example: two different people, one of whom is an atheist in the worst sense, the other a deeply religious person. Again, if both had the same illness and were treated with the same remedy, it might well happen that the religious person could be cured and the other not. These are things which will seem absurd to modern thinking — at least to the greater part of humanity — yet they are not.[12]

Here, in 1908, Rudolf Steiner described something as seeming absurd to contemporary thinking which in the meantime has become a recognized scientific fact. The wealth of research into the fields of immunology and psychoneuro-immunology has shown only too clearly that the immune system is determined and influenced by a person's emotional and mental identity. Uncertainty, fear and doubt work as immune depressants in the human organism, as do sadness and resignation. On the other hand, an idealistic attitude to life, an active religious life and a certain measure of joy in life bring about the exact opposite, stimulating the immune system.[13] For this reason, artistic and psychotherapeutic methods belong among the standard adjuvent therapies to operations, chemotherapy and radiotherapy in oncology units. But however interesting and stimulating the results of psychoneuro-immunology are, the bridge to real spirit cognition still remains undiscovered. Although people recognize the positive influence of emotional and mental activities upon the body, they fail to perceive the inner connections—which is why the materialistic perspective still holds its own. This can only be overcome through an anthroposophical understanding of the human being. And the key concept for understanding is that of the metamorphosis of the forces of growth into the forces of thinking. Rudolf Steiner and Ita Wegman described this metamorphosis in their book *Extending Practical Medicine*, in the following way:

> At the beginning of a human life on earth—most clearly so during the embryonic period—forces of the etheric body act as powers of form and growth. As life progresses, a part of these forces becomes emancipated from forming and growing activity, and is transformed into powers of thought, the very powers that create the shadowy thought world we have in ordinary consciousness.
>
> It is of the greatest importance to know that ordinary human powers of thought are refined powers of form and growth. A spiritual principle reveals itself in the formation and growth of the human organism. And as life progresses, this principle emerges as the spiritual power of thought.
>
> And this power of thought is only one part of the power of human forming and growth that is at work in the etheric. The other part remains faithful to the function it had at the beginning of human life. Human beings continue to develop further after formation and growth have reached an advanced stage—that is, some degree of conclusion; and it is because of this that the non-physical,

spiritual-etheric which lives and weaves in the organism can appear as the power of thinking in the further course of life.

The sculpting, forming power thus presents itself to imaginative perception as etheric-spiritual on the one hand, and on the other as the soul-content of thinking.[14]

At the threshold between conscious and unconscious thought-life stands the ego with its daily processes of learning and weighing things up, through which it becomes aware of its growth and formative forces metamorphosed into thoughts. These have a concrete inner relation to all phenomena of the world. There is after all no natural law which cannot be grasped by thinking, and which is not in some form involved in the growth and structure, the form and function of the human organism. And just as the etheric organism appears by day to be divided in two — into the conscious and unconscious life of thought and growth — so at night the whole etheric body is given over to its task of regenerating and caring for the life processes of the organism, though now with the after-effects of the thought processes of the past day. If, during the day, the ego has been living actively in this thought organism, with warmth and enthusiasm, then it brings strengthening, life-enhancing after-effects with it into the regenerative life of night. But if during the day our thinking has been sober, cool and unsatisfying for the soul, or just given over completely to the outer circumstances of life, it brings with it after-effects that result from a thinking rooted only in the physical world, that has lost its relation to living, ensouled and spiritual impulses.[15] Night by night, this has a destructive effect on the vitality of the organism, and can — depending on destiny, constitution and circumstances — lead to illness in some form or another. By day the etheric body works in a polarity — as both formative forces and thinking activity. At night, in contrast, it is active as a single, unified body of formative forces.

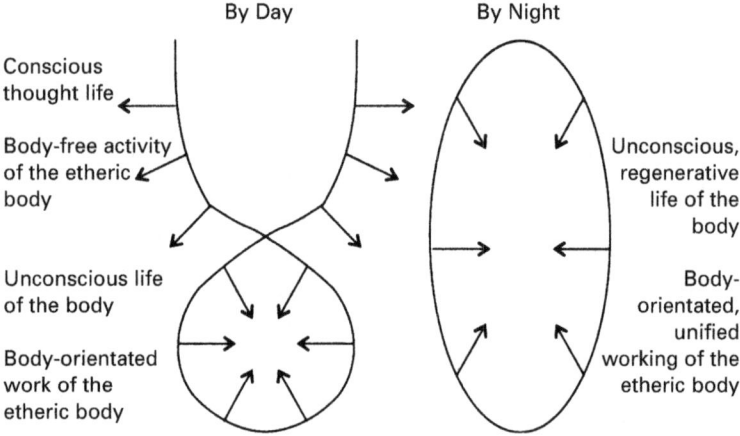

Rudolf Steiner describes the difference in effect on the body between pure thinking (e.g. in mathematics) and thought bound to sense perception:

> [There is] an entirely different influence exerted upon human nature by so-called 'sense-free' ideas than by those filled with sense-perception. Think for a moment of the difference between a man who likes mathematics and one who does not. [...] It is [...] of great use to the inner being of man to dwell on conceptions of what cannot be seen. Hence it is useful to have religious ideas, for these also relate to things which cannot be grasped with the hands nor have any connection with outer material things—in a word, with things that are sense-free. These are matters which will one day have a great influence on educational principles, when people develop more regard for the spiritual. [...] A person who has been used, from childhood on, to limit the compass of his thoughts to ones imbued wholly with sense-perceptions, will not so easily recover from illness (because his nervous system has been subject to more sickly conditions) as someone who has been accustomed to sense-free ideas. The more

people develop the habit of thinking independently of the sense-world, the easier it will be to cure them. When a person fell ill in ancient times, it was customary to place before them all kinds of symbolic figures, triangles and number-combinations. Beside the intrinsic value these possessed, the object was to uplift the person from a merely external vision of things. If I place a triangle before me and merely look at it, it has no particular value. But if on the other hand I see it as a symbol of the higher threefoldness of the human being, it becomes an idea which has a healing potency for the mind. [...] The science of the spirit will again become a powerful, universal remedy as it was formerly in the hands of Egyptian priests. In those times, though, it involved diminishing and suppressing the ego, which was achieved through the 'temple-sleep' ... A spiritual view of the world is a healing, curative one. [...] Those who perceive the spirit see a future in which the inner causes of illness will no longer exist for those able to create the inner and outer conditions necessary for developing spiritual wisdom. External causes will always exist, which can only be eradicated to the extent that an art of healing working out of the science of the spirit gains more and more ground. So we can see that the temple-sleep custom is not mysteriously unintelligible if we understand the working of the spirit.[16]

This theme — of spiritual science in the future becoming more and more necessary for humanity to remain healthy — is taken up again by Rudolf Steiner in 1920, in his lecture 'health-care as a social question'.[17] He confronts doctors with the great cultural task of increasingly becoming teachers of health in the broadest sense to people of their times, and to focusing their attention upon *preventing* illness. At the end of World War I, on 1 December 1918, he returns to this theme, but this time placing it into a much wider context.[18] He speaks about how hidden spiritual faculties which will increasingly be developed in the future are latent in the peoples of the East, central Europe and the West. He describes how in the East eugenic occultism will awaken—in other words an intimate knowledge of reproductive processes and the spiritual conditions underlying the way we incarnate. In the West, in contrast, a mechanistic occult faculty will develop, by means of which human beings will become intimately interwoven with the life of machines, learning to activate them through individual forces of soul and spirit. In regard to the occult faculties that will be developed in Europe, Rudolf Steiner speaks of a new, healing capacity:

> This hygienic, healing occult faculty is developing well—we will not have to wait too long for its appearance. This faculty will come to maturity simply through people developing insight into the fact that human life from birth to death progresses in a way identical to the course of an illness. Processes of illness are, in other words, only specific and radical transmutations of the normal, everyday process of life taking its course between birth and death; except that we bear within us not only the forces which make us ill, but also those which heal. And these healing forces, as every occultist knows, are exactly the same as those one makes use of in developing occult capacities, by transmuting them into knowledge. When transmuted into knowledge, the healing power innate in the human organism gives rise to occult knowledge. [...] for the moment that healing/occult faculties develop, people will no longer need external, material medicine; instead, it will become possible to treat psychically, prophylactically, in such a way as to prevent all illnesses which are not the result of karma, which are insusceptible to external influence. In this respect everything will alter. This seems nowadays like a mere fantasy, yet it is

something which will come about—and really very soon.[19]

Following a conscious path of development is a source of health and healing that every doctor and therapist must nowadays know. Thinking needs to be educated to truthfulness, feeling to the capacity for compassion and love, and willing to freedom—the kind of freedom also which is hardest to attain: from oneself and one's own self-involved needs.

But it may still sound incomprehensible that illnesses arising through karmic causes cannot be influenced. As doctors and therapists we are of course called upon to give of our best in these cases too—even especially so in such cases. And even if healing cannot result, in most cases some relief and improvement can be brought about. The patient can also be helped to live as well as possible with the illness, or to die with dignity. But behind this statement of Rudolf Steiner's lies hidden another quite fundamental, general law that adds considerably to what has so far been said. In the 'Curative Education Course',[20] Rudolf Steiner shows that between teacher and pupil a great pedagogical law is at work. All that lives in the ego of the teacher as presence of mind in every moment, has its effect on the pupil's astral body. All that takes place in the teacher's soul (astral body) affects the configuration of the pupil's etheric body. And what manifests in habits, ways of thinking, in the whole etheric conduct and manner of the teacher, has a formative influence on the pupil's physical body. But this law is not just valid for the teacher-pupil relationship. In our own lives we can recognize how our soul-state—whether we can keep a good mood or let things get to us—is dependent to a high degree on our ego being 'present' and aware. Equally, the basic tenor of our astral body, and the way we form our thoughts, handle our feelings, exercise our will in the alternation between work and rest, has a strong effect on the configuration of our etheric body and the formation of habits. And the physical body, finally, also reflects the enlivening processes which unfold in the etheric body. So how we feel lies to a great extent in our own hands — much more so than we usually feel is possible. Yet we can also experience the difficulty of getting our ego to extend its direct influence beyond the astral body, to affect the etheric and physical also. That is much harder to achieve. For the different human sheaths possess their own dynamic, and cannot be immediately affected. Why is it, otherwise, that many people can live their whole lives in a relatively healthy state even though their thinking and feeling is in a state of disorder? It is because they have a very healthy physical-etheric constitution at their disposal, that can for a long time resist the negative influences of their conscious soul-life. In such cases a longer period can elapse before the sheaths constituting the human being affect each other: we have to take repeated incarnations into consideration, and the transforming processes occurring between death and a new birth. Rudolf Steiner speaks about this in the lectures collected under the title *The Theosophy of the Rosicrucian*.[21] There he shows that the basic 'mood' and development of the astral body is dependent on the ego activity of a previous incarnation.

Attentiveness Interest in the world and in people	Ego	1st earthly life
Directing of thinking Cultivation of feeling Self-control in the will	Astral body	2nd life on earth
Habits Religious, artistic life	Etheric body	3rd life on earth
Physical deeds and behaviour	Physical body	4th life on earth

According to how we act and behave physically, destiny comes towards us again from outside ourselves, stimulating the ego's attentiveness and interest.

A person who passes his days in a joyful and life-affirming way, and who also knows how to use his thoughts, feelings and will impulses to cope with painful occurrences, forms for himself a disposition that will lead in his next life to a strong and active astral body, one ready to work on and assimilate things. A grumpy, withdrawn person on the other hand, who harbours particular bitternesses and gets stuck in certain grooves, prepares a future astral organism which gives the soul little flexibility and capacity for work. By the same token, it is the way in which we think, feel and act in one life that determines whether the etheric body can enliven the physical body and all its organ-functions in the next. And the forming of the physical body, including the tendencies to illness, inherited or otherwise, which it is born with, is likewise dependent on the nature of the etheric body in the previous life. The etheric body is, after all, the bearer of hereditary forces. Looked at in this way, we in fact carry with us at every moment of our lives the influences that shaped us as a result of our last four incarnations. The sheaths that constitute us, formed and impressed by karmic factors, surround us like a cloak of destiny which the ego has to wear and transform. This can be a somewhat crushing thought — for it dawns on us that we ourselves are to a large extent responsible for all that we usually think of in terms of illness and health. But this can also generate a great enthusiasm in us, and stimulate the will to rise to the challenge. And therein lies the enormous difference between our own times and the days of the 'temple sleep' in ancient Egypt. Human beings are not passive recipients of the doctor's healing art; rather, they can recognize their responsibility for, and their participation in their own health. But more specifically, we can find a modern metamorphosis of the ancient temple sleep through gaining knowledge about the connection between the powers of thinking and the regenerative activity of the organism, in which the fully conscious ego learns to take its own spiritual development in hand.

Ethical Questions as Threshold Questions

Medical activity always has the goal of being, or bringing about, good i.e. it is ethical. Yet public discussion, or investigation into ethics by appointed commissions, only takes place for situations in which the doctor clearly confronts a life and death threshold, or when practical intervention affects, or is an imposition on, a person's karma and destiny. This makes two things clear: on the one hand, threshold consciousness is beginning to stir in this area, and individuals sense their powerlessness to find their own way through the issues involved; and on the other, it shows how often in medical or therapeutic daily practice decisions are made simply because people have to behave according to the accepted therapeutic scheme, or because other colleagues do something in a particular way. The threshold boundary is not seen here with the same clarity, because people feel themselves to be on safe and proven ground. People therefore fail to ask their conscience what they are really doing. It is interesting to see how the view is beginning to make itself felt in literature on ethics—particularly medical ethics—that there cannot be any collective, i.e. general ethical norms in society. Rather, there is only the individual decision, which can be helped by advice, but in the end must be taken alone by the person affected—or as far as possible according to their wishes if they are no longer in a position to decide.[22] Looking at worldwide discussion on ethical questions in medicine, it is obvious that an unconscious, underlying experience of the threshold is rumbling, and pushing through into consciousness as people get to grips with these problems. The question is whether we can interweave the awakening and helpful insights of anthroposophy into our dialogue with our contemporaries. Above all, is it possible to bring knowledge of karma and reincarnation into conversation in such a way that ethical questions can connect with the facts of karma, and lead, through this, to a conscious experience of questions of destiny?[23] And how do we manage to bring *real* understanding to bear on a person's situation? What is organ donation? What, really, is the cause of someone's painful state of confusion in old age? What happens when a pregnancy is terminated? Here lie important questions of anthroposophical research that are in need of work.

(i) Questions about organ transplantation

It is often asked what anthroposophy's position is on organ transplants; and naturally one can only respond by saying: anthroposophy can stimulate individual thoughts and decisions, but it is not its purpose to make general judgements about this or that. For example, I have experienced a strong eleven year old girl offering her healthy kidney to her diseased identical twin, who could only have lived for a few weeks without the organ donation as she suffered from serious, progressive, cystic kidney disease. On the other hand, some people decline an organ donation and go consciously towards their death. Each question must be looked at in its own terms, and decided as far as possible by the sufferers themselves. What happens though with donated organs? Aren't the remains of etheric activity of the donor taken over into the recipient? In blood transfusion it is obvious how quickly the donated blood is worked through by the organism; and also when this process comes to an end — after six to ten weeks. With other organs, one knows that the biological activity of the donor's protein usually remains detectable for the recipient's lifetime. But this is not the same as a continuation of the donor's etheric activity. 'Pieces' cannot be cut out of the etheric. We are dealing, however, with a physical foreign body against which the organism defends itself, or which it largely accepts. Rudolf Steiner says about this that human substance can only affect the physical body of another human being.[24] This can be made clear with the example of renal transplantation: the small, pale, donor organ, empty of blood, and washed only by Ringer solution, and cooled to four degrees Celsius, is linked up to the circulation of the recipient. The organ immediately fills with blood, becomes larger, and within seconds is excreting urine. The fact that the astral body cannot yet take hold of the organ is demonstrated by the daily excretion of, at first, twenty litres of urine — because it is not yet concentrated. In a few days the urine volume decreases until the full concentration capacity is reached, and then only one to two litres are excreted daily — as in a healthy person. The assimilation of the new organ by the recipient's etheric body is shown, for example, in the transmutation of the nucleus-morphology gender of the kidney cells in cases when there was only a donor of the opposite sex available. After only fourteen days one can observe how the gender of the nuclei round the blood vessels in the transplanted kidney has become that of the recipient. In six to eight weeks the whole kidney has been transformed, and cells of the opposite sex (e.g. when a male kidney is transplanted into a woman) can no longer be demonstrated. What does remain a problem for the recipient however, is the physical donor-organ which cannot be completely transformed by the recipient. Etheric body, astral body and ego can use the organ as an instrument. For example, the etheric body can prepare urine, the astral body can concentrate the urine, and the ego integrates the organ into the metabolism of the whole organism in the way one would expect of a healthy kidney: e.g. playing a part in haemopoiesis, regulating the acid-base balance and the blood pressure. The donated organ can also get the same illness again that originally made the transplant necessary.

But why do so many people today want to make their organs available at death? What karmic factors are at work here? And if an organ is freely donated, why may the recipient not take grateful advantage of this, in spite of his struggle with the 'foreign protein'? Thus at the Crans-Montana Congress on transplant medicine it was reported euphorically:

> The third day of the meeting was completely given over to relaxing as well as to skiing and curling competitions [...] The sight of organ recipients who were able to take part in ski-races — an exciting moment which would never have taken place without anonymous organ donations — was as moving as it was enthusing: praise of transplantation became an Ode to Joy!

Questions such as that of living donors were also discussed at the Congress: 'In recent times, thanks to partial liver transplantation, living donation was discussed and carried out in individual cases.' Here we see then, a movement gathering momentum, one which is giving rise to new questions of destiny, and needs our participation and research. There is also the moving description by a journalist enthusiastic about transplant medicine, who is himself confronted by these questions through the death of his wife. He writes:

> Organ donation is also a question of trust. And only doctors can give this trust to those left behind. Only together can we really manage to enable the idea of saving lives with donated organs to be implemented. [...] For I believe that whoever is against organ transplants today denigrates life — does not protect it. Whoever inveighs against organ transplants on moral, ethical or religious grounds places himself in the moral wilderness, not recognising neighbourly love. Yet since my own wife Chantal Noelle Glogger died of a stroke in the early morning of 2 May on Zurich railway station, and I gave permission for her organs to be available for transplan-

tation, I have had doubts about the system of organ transplants. I am dubious about the manner and way in which Swiss doctors deal with the dead and their close ones.

There follows a detailed description of the events that took place between repeated confirmation of the clinical death (compare this with brain death on p. 76) of his wife and her transportation to the transplant centre. What he missed here, and what he challenges the doctors for, is a consciousness of the dignity of death and of the reality of human relationships in death also.

Thanks to the organs of my wife, four people can today live better lives [...] As I said: I will continue to fight on for organ transplantation, with my journalistic tools. But I am horrified by the inhuman, degrading way organ donors and their relatives are brushed aside.[25]

Such examples make clear that it is not only questions of knowledge about the human being that need to be discussed — which are different in the case of each different organ — but, above all, new questions of destiny and of how one works with dying and with death. However, the central ethical question is always whether we really know what we are doing.

With regard to the question of what organ transplantation really is, I gained great help from reading a lecture given by Steiner in London — 'Experiences of the Human Soul in Sleep and after Death in the Spiritual World'.[26] Here Rudolf Steiner describes a dramatic alteration in the preparation of the earthly body, from the perspective of the spiritual world:

Since ancient times of earthly evolution, it has been as I today described it. The human being prepares the spiritual seed of his own physical body, which he takes over when he steps forth into his new life on earth. Now however, since the Christ-Michael leadership has begun, people will be increasingly able to make another important decision before they come down to earth.[...] With the increasing spread of spiritual knowledge on the Earth and with man's growing experience within himself of universal human love, the following possibility will arise for mankind in coming time. At the point of descending into a new earthly life, a person will be able to say to himself: 'This is the body I have been preparing; yet, having sent it down to Earth and having now received my karma into the ether-body which I have drawn together from the Cosmos, I see how it is with this karma. Through something that I did in former lives I see that I have gravely hurt some other human being.' For we are always in the danger of hurting others through the things we do. The light of judgement as to what we have done to another person will be particularly vivid at this moment when we are still living only in our ether-body, having not yet put on the physical. Here too in future time the light of Michael will be working, and the love of Christ. And we shall then be enabled to bring about a change in our decision—namely to give to the other person the body we have been preparing, while we ourselves take on the body prepared by the person we have injured. Such is the mighty transition which will be taking place from now onward in the spiritual life of human beings. It will be possible for us, by our own decision, to enter into the body prepared perforce by another human soul to whom we once did previous harm; he on the other hand will be enabled to enter into the body we prepared. What we are able to achieve on earth will thus bring about karmic compensation in quite another way than heretofore. We human beings shall be able even to exchange our physical bodies. Indeed, the earth could never reach her goal if this did not take place; mankind would never grow into a single whole. In preparation for future planetary embodiments of the earth, a time must come in earthly evolution when it will be impossible for one individual to enjoy things on the earth at the expense of another. As in a plant the single leaf or petal feels itself a member of the whole and shares — pictorially speaking — in the weal and woe of the whole plant, so must a future come for the planet earth when one human being will not want to enjoy happiness at the expense of the whole, but the human being will feel a member of mankind. And it will be the true spiritual counterpart of this when we shall learn to prepare the physical body even for one another.

What Rudolf Steiner describes as a fact beginning in the Michael Age in the spiritual world — does it not have its materialistic reflection in the practice of blood and organ donation in our century?

In the face of these questions, the more people open themselves to a knowledge of the threshold to the spiritual world, the easier it will be for them to answer boundary questions of this nature for themselves. Organ donation will then not be demanded because of a fear of death, but perhaps only because one wants still to achieve something quite important on earth, for the sake of which one is prepared to take on board organ donation and all the medical problems this may involve. Of course, there are quite different karmic consequences resulting from such a decision than exist when someone in a similar situation sees it as their karma *not* to be able to do any more on earth, and therefore rejects further such physical help. Ethical questions, thus understood, do not lead to right or wrong, either/or; On the contrary, they lead a person towards consciously taking hold of and forming their destiny. Questions of ethics are questions of destiny.

(ii) Confusion in Old Age—Standing at the Threshold of Death

In severe illnesses or comatose states, the question about their meaning arises in a particularly painful way. No one wishes to have to live through these sorts of circumstances themselves, and therefore no one wishes them on another—indeed, there is an instinctive tendency in many people to help the other by ending the suffering. Not least due to this feeling, the ethical discussion on euthanasia has arisen. Here too one cannot arrive at impressions and feelings based on reality without studying spiritual-scientific facts. What does it mean karmically, for example, when a person who has always done their work energetically and conscientiously, who always thought that he did not need to depend on others, and was always the one who gave, must in old age live through a protracted period, years even, when he needs to be cared for; maybe even needs spiritual help because he is confused and has lost his memory? From the earthly point of view his experience is unconscious—from the spiritual, however, very conscious—of what a blessing it is that other people are there for him, and that, as a human being he can learn to accept help, and in doing so have quite different experiences to those of giving help. To say nothing of the possibility that is given to those karmically connected to the person, to think through their connection to him in quite a new way and to balance out various aspects that were unresolved until then. Rudolf Steiner's 'Leading Thoughts' can be a great help in pondering these questions.[27] For it is shown there how the ego of the human being is not only active in the head area as a consciously self-reflecting, sensory ego but is also present as ego impulse ('ich-haft') in the rhythmic system and the metabolic limb system. Although not partaking of waking consciousness, this presence is very active in experiencing, through dreams and sleep, what happens to the body. From this point of view, the concept of brain death is a total misconception. For the ego presence in the rhythmic system and the metabolic limb system is still there. A 'silent personality'—as it was once beautifully expressed in a newspaper—has appeared. The awake, reactive, everyday ego that has its consciousness reflected in the nervous system of the senses is extinguished. But all the more deeply do the other two centres of consciousness perceive: the dreaming feeling that is bound to the rhythmic system, and the sleeping will. This point of view of the threefold nature[28] of the human being with three centres of ego consciousness (awake thinking, dreaming feeling and sleeping willing) also leads to an understanding of so-called brain death that is in harmony with human dignity.

Things must be thought through anew from this aspect too, when the decision to ventilate a comatose patient, or not, lies before one; also in the case of a so-called brain-dead woman who carries a child within her that is alive and moving. Death can only be spoken of in a spiritual-scientific sense when, after laying aside the entire physical body, images of the past life begin to unfurl as the etheric body disperses. This release of the etheric body can only take place when the heartbeat and breathing stop and the separation of the soul and spirit from the body has taken place. Then the etheric body ceases its mediating between the soul-spirit and the physical body, and after the review of life in the first three days and nights after death has taken place, withdraws to the far breadths of the world.[29] Some people who are more sensitive can quite tangibly experience the presence of the soul-spirit being of the ill person, even when he is deeply asleep or in a coma. The moment of death, however, which may have come after weeks of waiting, is different in every case. It is quite clear from Rudolf Steiner's descriptions of death, and life after death, that we are dealing with far-reaching initiation experiences; with standing on the threshold of death between the physical and the spiritual worlds; with a wealth of soul and spirit experiences. This is also very clear from the descriptions of patients who have returned to full consciousness from a comatose state or after resuscitation. Looking at these questions can particularly illuminate why suffering an illness as such, as a physical experience, is an invaluable spiritual gain. For everything that the ego experiences unconsciously in the will realm of the metabolism, becomes conscious after death through the help of the beings in the planetary sphere of Mercury, and turns into gladdening, encompassing knowledge accompanying the person throughout all the further life after death.[30]

Insights of this kind lead as well to a quite new understanding of the procedures in intensive care units in hospitals. Particularly as we know that despite all the technology of ventilation and infusion, death can come at any moment in an intensive care unit, if a person's life is really at an end. Medical procedures in intensive care can give the ill person the physical support which enables the higher members to keep themselves in the physical body. However, the life of these higher members in the body can never be 'compelled'. If the moment of death has come for someone, the rhythmic system gives up, the heartbeat stops or another unforeseeable complication sets in, and despite all medical art and technology, death cannot be held back. This is often not made clear enough, so that many people harbour the illusion nowadays that doctors can voluntarily prolong life. It is far more in their power to help end life voluntarily, by withholding help—with the corresponding consequences in destiny. The fact that many people today become so old and must often undergo states of suffering in old age at the threshold between the sense and the spirit worlds, may also lead us to ask whether modern humanity's yearning to experience the threshold clearly is manifesting here—even if this can no longer take place with awake, earthly consciousness. So we find ourselves increasingly faced with the task of accompanying such confused or 'silent' personalities with particular love and spiritual understanding. After death, these experiences become conscious and help prepare a spiritually-oriented succeeding life on earth.[31]

Such understanding can also allow us to ask in which 'school' someone has already been learning, who is born highly gifted and needs little help to make the most varied talents conscious, and use them. Something that has been endured unconsciously in the will, on the bodily level, in one life, becomes conscious experience and ability in the next. It is quite obvious that it has become necessary in our century to grow conscious of standing at the threshold. However, because this happens too little, ever more borderline experiences and threshold situations arise, which stimulate the people involved to think about questions of this kind. Thus threshold consciousness is awakened through painful experiences.

> [...] For the whole future of mankind depends on human beings learning really to live with the spiritual world as naturally as they live with the physical on the earth. Mankind must learn to be at home again in the spiritual world as it was in the beginning, in primeval time. Only by doing so shall we be helping mankind's future. In the true sense we must understand the word of Christ: 'My kingdom is not of this world'.[32]

(iii) On the Termination of Pregnancy[33]

This is not the right place to explore this controversial and socially difficult theme in any depth. Conversations about the abortion laws do show, however, the great extent to which, here at the gateway of birth as well, consciousness of standing at the threshold of the spiritual world is darkened. These laws, particularly, reveal with great clarity the possibilities and limitations which arise in proposing collective, ethical norms today.[34]

Rudolf Steiner repeatedly declared that there is one word which Ahriman finds it unbearable to listen to. It is the word: 'unborn-hood' (Ungeborenheit).[35] The questions and pain that move those who are witness to, or are in the field of abortion, direct the consciousness towards the world of the unborn. Dying is connected with people's egoism, whereas being born is linked to their altruism — a quality which Ahriman flees. At birth it is still totally uncertain who and what comes towards us. The benevolence, love and devotion of the surrounding world are called upon.

At this point I would like to quote Frits Wilmar.[36] He followed the debate on the revision of the abortion law with great interest and warm involvement until his death last year. It was far from his nature to assume a judgemental position. Rather, the whole soul drama of the materialistic age lay before his gaze, a drama which must struggle through guilt and pain to threshold consciousness. As a doctor he felt himself duty-bound to make the results of spiritual scientific research on pre-birth life and human development available, and to allow this knowledge to gently clarify and illuminate modern consciousness. He writes in his excellent book *Vorgeburtliche Menschwerdung* ('the pre-birth evolving human being'):

> For reasons that have to do with its past earthly destiny, [...] the soul gains the impulse for a new life after remaining and working in the 'spirit lands' for a long time. Under the guidance of the higher beings of the spirit realm, it turns itself gradually towards a future existence on earth. [...] At the beginning of this process, the spirit-soul of the human being has to experience how the spirit seed of the physical body is taken from it by higher powers, how the spirit seed distances itself from the soul and begins to approach the earth under the guidance of higher powers. It begins to concentrate itself as an energy

being. In a way it diminishes in breadth. During this stage, the consciousness of the human soul-spirit, which is still in the spirit realm, changes both in content and direction. It now begins to experience itself as a single being again. This experience is then quickly filled with all that the previous earth life contributed as imperfections and faults. The spiritual hierarchies then form the new soul body (astral body) of the individuality, in the sense that everything which was rejected in some way by the cosmic order and stored in the soul world as 'substance' in beings of particular spiritual hierarchies, is embodied from now on in the human being for the coming earthly life. It is altered in such a way that it contains within it the impulses and forces to balance out the imperfections of the previous earth life. These impulses will come towards the human ego during its life on earth, partly from within as physical constitution; and partly from without as destiny — for the most part in a way quite beyond the grasp of normal waking consciousness.[37]

On the question of in-vitro fertilisation, which has been successfully carried out thousands of times since 1978, Frits Wilmar writes:

Such successful imitations of the earliest embryonic stages could be balanced against the ideas developed in this book. It could be possible in this way to reach an evaluation of these processes, ones partly formed according to arbitrary human wish. One should ask oneself how the course of these children's lives, whose earliest embryonic stages were artificially manipulated, will develop. To answer such questions one must be prepared to observe over longer periods of time, at least far into the adulthood of the individuals concerned.[38]

He counters this attitude of arbitrary intervention in the threshold of birth — in the two wholly opposite aspects of pregnancy termination and artificial fertilisation — with the results of spiritual research and his investigations of the human being. Frits Wilmar enters into conversation with his contemporaries and gives us an outstanding example of how we can realize the intentions of anthroposophy—to waken threshold consciousness in individual people, and so be able to help individuals acquire responsibility and truly find themselves. At this point, I would also like to mention Max Hofmeister's work[39] which provides a basis for posing questions connected with conception and contraception.[40]

Only a few instances of Rudolf Steiner speaking on the subject of termination of pregnancy are known. However, in the circular letter to young doctors of 11 March 1924 he gives basic indications to do with the karmic reality of this subject:

> To the question of whether one is interfering with the karmas of mother and child if *one saves the mother*[41] through an abortion, we can reply that we can hardly speak of an intervention in their karmas, since although both karmas will, for a short time, be directed to other channels, they will soon be brought back to the right direction by the natural course of events. On the other hand, the karma of the person doing the operation is strongly affected. And he has to ask himself whether he really wants to do something which brings him into karmic connections which would not otherwise have existed. But questions of this kind depend upon the particular circumstances and cannot be answered in general, like many other things of purely soul-dimensions in cultural life, which constitute an intervention in karma and which can lead to serious and tragic conflicts.[42]

We know of no indications from Rudolf Steiner on voluntary pregnancy termination. This does not involve questions of medical necessity, but in each case there is a tragedy of destiny which is hard to judge externally. In the face of this kind of tragedy, one thing only will be effective: knowledge of the spiritual, of reincarnation and the reality of karma. Our task is to bring the consciousness of these realities into modern culture.[43]

What for example would doctors advise, and how would they fight for the life of every child, if they realised the karmic repercussions for themselves of pregnancy termination? The basic question of ethics must always be: Do I know what I'm doing? Can I stand by the consequences and accept responsibility?

In his writings on the results of Rudolf Steiner's spiritual scientific research, Max Hofmeister directs us to a current topic, one I will now deal with as it has a direct relation to the healing, hygienic occultism previously described. Rudolf Steiner says that we will not have to wait long for this faculty to appear. This means that this faculty, which is connected to the spiritualisation of thinking, must precede the development of both eugenic and mechanistic occult faculties, so that the latter two may be channelled in the right directions. It seems that development in the East and the West has proceeded more rapidly but, due to the insufficient development of hygienic occultism as a force in the middle, in Europe, appears first in materialistic distortions. So, in the East, (China and Japan) contraception and the practice of abortion, regulated by law, stand in contrast to the ever more perfect world of machines in the West, which increasingly intrudes into the souls and spirits of people who, day-in, day-out, are in 'dialogue' with computers or allow their souls to merge with entertainment technology. Max Hofmeister writes about this in his commentaries on Rudolf Steiner's indications:

> If one tries to live into the questions of one's fellow human beings on the basis of a spiritual view of the world, such as anthroposophy provides, one begins to

realise that these questions are the first pre-condition for attaining the faculty of eugenic occultism, through which it will be possible and permissible in the future to regulate conception. Then the question of whether parents are free to make a decision to allow conception to take place or not, will resolve itself. Nowadays we quite clearly find ourselves in an interim phase of development which is turbulent and chaotic in all areas of life. Children do not reach their originally intended parents, due to the many abortions and preventions of conception. The impression that Rudolf Steiner had of human seeds shooting here and there in haste through the astral realm in order to find a somewhat suitable parental pair for their incarnation, can be said to point to this and seems to be the prevalent state today...[44]

To close, a reminder of the task that Rudolf Steiner speaks of in his lecture in Dornach on 13 March 1921:[45]

But just seek everywhere in civilised language for a practicable word for 'unborn-hood' (Ungeborenheit). The word 'immortal' turns up everywhere, but we have no word for the state of being 'unborn'. We need that word; it must be just as valid a word as the word immortal today. This reveals the extent of Ahrimanisation of our modern civilisation; one of the most significant symptoms of the Ahrimanising of modern civilisation is that we have no word for this 'not being born'. For just as we do not simply dissolve into earth when we 'die', neither do we exist only from the moment of birth or conception. We need a word which points clearly to pre-existence. We must not undervalue the significance which lies in such a word.

You see, my dear friends, no matter how acutely one thinks, there is something in you, something in man, of an intellectualizing nature; but the very moment the thought is expressed in a word, even the very moment the word is only thought, as in the words of a meditation, then that word is imprinted into the ether of the cosmos. Thought, as such, does not imprint itself into the ether of the cosmos, otherwise we could never become free beings in the sphere of pure thought. We are bound the moment something imprints itself. We are not made free through the word, but through pure thought. (You can read about this in my *Philosophy of Freedom*.) The word imprints itself into the cosmic ether.

Now just consider this fact of which the science of initiation is fully aware: that because in civilised languages there is no word 'unborn-hood', this state of not being born which is so important for humanity, is not imprinted into the cosmic ether. Everything of such a nature imprinted into the cosmic ether terrifies Ahrimanic beings: everything imprinted into the world ether that is connected with things coming to life, with the childhood and youth of human beings. Ahrimanic beings can very easily bear the word 'immortality' being inscribed in the world ether; they are quite pleased, because immortality means that they can start a new Creation with man, and keep a firm grasp on humanity. It does not irritate Ahrimanic beings, as they shoot through the cosmic ether playing their game with man, to find that immortality is trumpeted from all pulpits; that does not irritate them, it pleases them. But it is a terrible shock for them if they find the word unborn-hood inscribed in the world ether; it extinguishes the light in which these Ahrimanic beings move. Then they can go no further, they lose their direction, they feel as though they are falling into an abyss, a bottomless pit. You can see from this that it is an Ahrimanic deed which restrains humanity from speaking of unborn-hood.[...] It is actually nothing less than conflict with Ahrimanic powers that we must take upon ourselves.

Symptoms of the Unconscious Crossing of the Threshold

On 1 May 1919, Rudolf Steiner speaks at length, for the first time, about humanity's unconscious crossing of the threshold.[46] What are the signs, the symptoms, from which this crossing can be deduced? We know from the descriptions of the path of initiation in the book, *How To Know Higher Worlds*, that the loosening of thinking, feeling and willing from the sovereignty of the ego in the physical body, their urge to separate from each other, is a significant sign of the crossing of the threshold. This means that a strong effort is needed on the part of the ego for it to hold these soul forces together on the other side in a new and purely spiritual way. This effort is necessary each time the human being consciously spends time pursuing a path of knowledge of the supersensible world:

> This is the significant and inwardly active experience we go through after crossing the threshold: experiencing the inner life through ego activity carried to the highest degree, in order to hold together the soul forces, thinking, feeling, willing, when they have been separated. Here enters the fear felt by present day man through his lack of courage — fear of real supersensible knowledge, fear of this intense degree of soul activity. Modern man would like all soul activity to run its course just in response to the external world, and to be effective there. Such active inner life does not lie in the nature of modern man, but it is something that must be increasingly developed in preparation for the future [...] Our consciousness is enhanced when we cross the threshold, and when we perceive the threefoldness of the human soul in the supersensible worlds.
>
> Something similar, but naturally given and not conscious, is being experienced by the whole of mankind at

the present time—a cosmic historic experience. An unconscious process which is experienced by all mankind passes unnoticed unless studied consciously through spiritual science.[...] This it is which is being enacted in the unconscious of humanity as a whole at the present time, which must be explained by spiritual science, and which also proves the necessity of spiritual science for people nowadays. For this crossing of the threshold must not remain in the unconscious.[47]

This spiritual-scientific fact described by Rudolf Steiner, that human beings have crossed the threshold to the spiritual world unconsciously, goes hand in hand with a symptom visible throughout humanity today which can only be understood when conscious threshold experience has been gone through: namely, the experience of the separation of thinking, feeling and willing, and the necessity of working anew on holding them together. It is just this point that is the main characteristic of the scientific life of our century: we have a science that is proud of the fact that it has separated itself from feeling and willing, i.e. is objective. Separation of thinking, feeling and willing has taken place for a long time already—without its importance being recognised. On the one hand, this century has witnessed ever more terrible world wars and unimaginable outbreaks of human brutality and bestiality. Here the will has clearly freed itself from feeling, and follows the body-bound urges and desires, uncontrolled by thinking and feeling. The great problems of the present: science without responsibility, and a growing lovelessness in the social realm, are nothing more than the symptoms of this separation of thinking, feeling and willing, and the incapacity of humanity to deal correctly with it. Thus, given this general state of humanity, each separate person needs to face up to the task of becoming aware of the reality of the unconscious crossing of the threshold, and of preparing for its conscious crossing by following paths of self-development. But this means, at the same time, 'recognizing death in its significance for all of human life'.[48]

Thus the most important task for modern humanity is a question of will: of facing this challenge of unconsciousness while both standing at and crossing the threshold; and directing our own development along corresponding lines.

On The Renewal of the Mysteries

In the second volume of the biography *Wer war Ita Wegman?* ('who was Ita Wegman?')[49] there is an entry from a notebook of Ita Wegman's in connection with the Arlesheim Doctors' Conference of October 1936. This entry is of central importance for the development of the Medical Section and the question of the renewal of the Mysteries:

> [There were] two questions that I put to Dr. Steiner; I can even give the exact time when I did so. The first question was in England after the Penmaenmawr Summer School: Why is the Mystery element in medicine no longer placed in the foreground and moulded in a clear form? Why must medical courses be given in such an intellectual way? Dr. Steiner said: 'That has to be so, because the conditions for doing it differently are not yet there; that you ask these questions is of great importance.' In October/November 1923 he then gave us the many Mystery lectures: the Michaelmas, Christmas, Easter and St. John Imagination lectures in which the cosmic healing art was discussed. The Christmas Foundation meeting took place and new life flowed into the Anthroposophical Society. A real start was made to form the medical work differently. Let me remind you of the lectures given to young doctors and medical students. The Mystery principle is that one learns to think pictorially, that events in the whole universe are taken in in pictures; likewise healing in the cosmos and healing in the microcosmos — which is only a picture of the macrocosmos. In meditations these pictures must then be brought together.
>
> My second question to Dr. Steiner was shortly before his illness in September 1924. I asked: 'Is it not possible to found a medical Mystery school?'
>
> Rudolf Steiner's answer was: 'That is not so easy, that

must be willed by the spiritual world and there must be people there who want to receive it.'

After a few days, he told me that he had asked the spiritual being Mercury-Raphael, and had received an affirmative answer. He was given the task of renewing old customs that once took place in ancient holy sites under the guidance of Mercury-Raphael. The task of seeking human souls borne by the spirit, who had a sense for such deeds and who wanted to give ear to the words of Raphael, would fall upon me.

We then made a quite small start. Thus the seed for the Raphael School was laid.

My dear friends, that was important; all the healing principles in the various Mysteries gathered together in one school. Michael and Raphael working together!

Unfortunately it could not be, one could literally feel the earth resisting. Earth and human beings did not yet want such an immense spirituality. Dr. Steiner then left this earthly working voluntarily, his illness was only maya. And human beings remained alone and fell into the old evil of evaluating everything intellectually and judging all through reason. The Anthroposophical Society was shaken to its roots. Karmic connections were brought into disarray. Human beings had not yet the maturity to receive so much spirituality; or else — and that is the positive aspect of dissension and fighting — retarding forces (which are also often necessary), realising that sufficient maturity was not yet available, set themselves against the course of events in order to prevent spiritual imperfections arising in spiritual development. That is how it seems.

... We have the longing for a Mystery medicine. But we cannot just proceed with what was started. We must try to prepare ourselves again, to awaken in ourselves a spirit recollection of what was once present in the old Mysteries. I will do all in my power to help with this.

> To make clear who the Mercury-Raphael being is.
> Michael helps human beings in their battle to change nature consciousness into self-awareness, to create [the latter]. Michael is there, the spiritual, the cosmic healer, working on the head. Mercury-Raphael stands beside the human being, working on his respiratory system, just as Michael's flaming sword is forged from cosmic iron and with this force fights the nature consciousness of human beings that wishes to rise up; and magics forth the conscious awareness of self.[50]

Nine years earlier in 1927, Ita Wegman described her situation, as leader of the Medical Section during the first large conference of doctors after Rudolf Steiner's death, as follows:

> I was faced with the need to represent Rudolf Steiner's method, which was a matter of course for me; but on the other hand, it was not possible for me to foresee how far I would succeed in this. One needs time to grow into the method, time to allow the healing method to ripen in oneself so as to stand on one's own two feet and be able to proceed. And the many difficulties which arose in the Society did not, unfortunately, exactly make things easy for the Medical Section. It was then unable to do justice to all the demands that were placed on it; it could not, for example, carry out scientific work that related to developments in the wider world, as was rightly expected of it. Thus for a long time the work had to be more preparatory, collecting more experience, in order to grasp with deepened understanding all the indications that Dr. Steiner had given for the healing of illness. Healing was the main thing for us at first, and also that we could gain conviction that the experiences we gathered could provide a basis upon which the work could be carried out into the world.
> In many places work continued in this way, and

experience was exchanged and collected whenever possible. Gradually one gained a better overview through this, and the deficiencies that were still there could be recognised and corrected. This then led to the opportunity for experimental testing: to find out on the one hand where the causes of these deficiencies lay, and on the other, to strengthen what Dr. Steiner had laid before us as facts from scientific research. At the same time we should begin to carry the work out into the world. For the outer world has gradually become aware of us through our successes in healing and asks for insight and explanation. As a result of this, the moment has arrived that requires us to draw the work together even more than before, and to consolidate it in order to be ready for all the demands that the outer world makes of us...[51]

From the old pre-Christian Mysteries (for instance the Egypto-Babylonian, the Samothracian, Greek and the great Hibernian) we know through Rudolf Steiner's descriptions, and preserved historical documents, how the cultural, political and practical life of nations was guided and determined by these Mystery sites. The awakening of historical and philosophical consciousness from 800 BC onwards went hand in hand with the decadence or closure of these old Mystery sites; and the secularisation of science already mentioned began. For the first time, democratic, republican and anarchic strivings arose. The prophecy of the St. John's Gospel began to fulfil itself increasingly — as it was not given for an elite group of rulers, but spoken for each single person: 'Ye will know the truth and the truth will make ye free.' With this the most intimate secrets of the old Mysteries were brought into the open: the path of knowledge towards freedom, and the attainment of individual freedom as an individual human being. The inscription on the temple of Apollo at Delphi says: 'Know yourself as a human being', and another reads: 'Nothing too much' — i.e. 'Moderation in all things'. These two demands, to recognise oneself as a human being and to find the middle between all extremes was the most essential, central teaching that came out of the ancient Mysteries.

How can we now approach the question which, in the light of these old, infinitely wise cultures, can lead to the renewal of the Mysteries? Has the wisdom of the Mysteries not already poured itself out into the whole human cultural life of today, in the sense that anyone can, in their own way, find their path to truth and freedom? Isn't it so that human beings have taken their destiny into their own hands now and, in the most varied ways, themselves elected the people to whom they give the task of leadership in local community and State? Quite certainly, a renewed Mystery culture cannot be one which revives old forms of spiritual supremacy or secret knowledge, by means of which those who are unknowledgeable may be ruled. That would be a retrograde step and would ignore the fact that Christ has been on earth. The new Mysteries must respect the human ego that is attaining its majority. That means too, however, that human future will depend increasingly on individuals beginning to interest themselves in the greater matters which are of concern to all humanity, and becoming aware of their own co-responsibility. The new Mysteries are Mysteries of the Will, Mysteries to do with the forms of social life. At the basis of these lies an individual's free decision to place his will at the service of the community.

Thus a renewed Mystery culture can only follow directly from the Christ Event, which Rudolf Steiner, through this very insight, ever and again called the Mystery of Golgatha or the Christ Mystery. This was a deed. It was a sacrifice brought for the freeing and redemption of human beings. The followers of Christ therefore recognise only demands of the human will, which are so difficult to fulfil: Love your enemies, Do good to those that hate you, Bless those that curse you. Qualities of will such as faith, love and hope are demanded. In these, however, lies the future. In his public lecture on the Apocalypse of St. John, in Nuremberg on 17 June 1908, Rudolf Steiner says on this theme:

> The more individualised man becomes the more he can become a bearer of Love. Where the blood links people together they love because they are led to what they should love. When we are granted individuality, when we tend and nurture the divine spark within us, then the impulses of love, the waves of love, pass from person to person out of the free heart. And thus with this new impulse man has enriched the old bond of love that is bound to the blood-tie. Love passes over gradually into spiritual love which flows from soul to soul and which will ultimately encompass all humanity in a common bond of brother- and sister-love. [...] Earlier initiation was directed to the past, to age-old wisdom; Christian initiation reveals the future to the one who is to be initiated. That is a necessity; man is to be initiated not only in wisdom or in feelings, but in his will. For then he knows what he is to do, he can set himself a goal for the future. Ordinary everyday people set themselves aims for the afternoon, for the evening or the morning; the spiritual person is able, out of spiritual principles, to set himself distant aims which pulse through his will and make his forces quicken. To set goals for humanity means in the true, highest sense, in the sense of the original Christ principle, to grasp Christianity esoterically. In this way it was grasped by the one who wrote down the great principle of the initiation of the will—the writer of the Apocalypse. We misunderstand the Apocalypse if we do not understand it as the impulse given for the future, for action and deed.[52]

In order for us to learn to *live* the Apocalypse of St. John, as the impulse-giver of deeds, anthroposophical spiritual science is necessary. It places itself as mediator between the old and the new Mysteries. Through his methodically developed spiritual vision, Rudolf Steiner was able to put into words accessible to modern consciousness the deepest wisdom of the old Mysteries and the instructions for schooling in self-development. He was also able to form the pictorial language of the Apocalypse into thoughts and aims in such a way that modern people can take them into their decisions and will impulses. This thought and spirit bridge-building between the old and new Mysteries is the historical deed of Rudolf Steiner. Through it, the event of the mid-point of earth evolution, the Christ Event, could be grasped as a conscious fact in the life of thought itself. And anthroposophy could become a preparer of the way and a herald of the reappearance of the Christ in the etheric realm (to which the life of thought belongs). At the same time, however, the scientific basis for the renewal of the Mysteries is also created: namely, the cardinal law that in these new Mysteries we have to do with the Mystery of the Will, the preparation of the future, the deed. In describing this new Christian Mystery culture that will lead humanity into a future worthy of human beings, Rudolf Steiner could lead on from Goethe and, in particular, from Goethe's fairy tale, in which the Mystery motto for the future is heard when the old man with the lamp says: 'A single person does not help, only one who unites with many others at the right time.'[53] In other words, the individual, the separate, single person — which was the evolutionary goal of the old Mysteries, right up to the birth of the ego at the Mystery of Golgatha — is no longer of use in the future. What alone helps is for single, individual human beings to unite in the right kind of common striving, and at the right time. Whoever grasps this new Mystery motif can understand why Rudolf Steiner thought it so important, from 1902 onwards when he took over the German section of the Theosophical Society, to inaugurate and nurture forms of community building. Even if some things did not succeed — such as, for example, the attempt to found a society for Theosophical methods and art[54] — it never prevented him from continuing to work in this direction. Ever more people came to him who were looking for indications and help in renewing different professional fields of work, and the new professional ideals all had community-building effects: in education, medicine, nursing, curative education, the priesthood, agriculture, artistic activities and science. People of each particular professional group renewed their professional ideals and so united in their striving to integrate this activity with social reality.

And yet we are still at the very beginning of realising a new mystery culture, and have great difficulty, individually as well as socially, in understanding what it is all about. It is therefore all the more important to look to the great personalities who had already grasped this impulse, taken it up and, as far as possible, made it reality. After Rudolf Steiner, the first such personalities were his two closest co-workers, Marie Steiner and Ita Wegman. At the beginning of the century already, Marie Steiner posed the question about a specifically Christian esoteric path of schooling in the West, and so became the co-founder and nurturer of all anthroposophical work. It was Ita Wegman who in the time after the fire of the first Goetheanum — New Year's Eve 1922 — asked Rudolf Steiner about the renewal of the Mysteries, which led to the Christmas Foundation meeting and the founding of the School of Spiritual Science as a public esoteric school. A further answer to this question was Rudolf Steiner's decision to write the book *Extending Practical Medicine* together with Ita Wegman. We know the salient points about their way of working on this book, thanks to a few descriptions by Rudolf Steiner and the teasing out of connections provided in Volume I of the Wegman biography.[55] The will to work together which freely united teacher and pupil was the most important basis for their collaboration. In 1932, medical students asked the question: 'What does the future have to offer us?' Ita Wegman answered: 'The question can be put quite differently: How can I form the future?'

This phrase—that we should not ask what the future holds in store for us, but rather how we can form the future—shows that Ita Wegman herself was working in full consciousness within the will stream of the Mystery culture renewed by Christianity. She stands before us as a human being who has completed the transition from the old to the new Mysteries in deep, inner insight, and who lived and worked accordingly. Demanding more and more new knowledge cannot be our main aim nowadays. It is our task, instead, to actually realise and make fruitful for development a small portion of what is already available in the world and within life as insight and knowledge. In active doing, in making real a wisdom which is individually recognised, heartfelt and extends into loving action, lies the being of the new Mystery. It is described for our epoch by Rudolf Steiner in his lectures on the Apocalypse of St. John.

In reading the Apocalypse, one is shattered by the immense visions of evil, the horrors of human nature's bestial outbursts that at first seem so irreconcilable with the revelation of the Christ Principle. Here we push through to the central secret of the new Mysteries, that are in fact Mysteries of the Will, of doing, of deed: the secret of evil. It is one of the deepest riddles of Christianity that the Mystery of Golgatha, the Passion, involves torture, martyrdom and violent death accompanied by hate, mockery and spite— things that all reveal the evil possibilities of human nature.

This riddle can only be resolved if we recognise in the ego-nature of human beings the double-edged sword of which the Apocalypse speaks. This double edge is connected with the ego's capacity for freedom: the faculty of deciding between two possibilities so that a middle path can become visible between caprice and compulsion, pride and self-sacrifice, waste and meanness, foolhardiness and cowardice etc. It is not a choice between good and evil but rather a continuous struggle for a state of balance between two extremes, the Luciferic evil and the Ahrimanic evil.[56] And so we should not be astonished that all the possibilities of deviation, and the horrors which will still arise in the course of humanity's evolution as a consequence of ego endowment, are already anticipated in the images of the Apocalypse. They should not lead us to despair but help to fire our will, to help us to be ready to act in such a way as to serve the progress of humanity's evolution.

Even if, in the transition from one great cultural epoch to the next, it is often only a small group of people who truly recognise and preserve the purpose of humanity's development, this does not mean that other straying souls may not gradually attain new evolutionary possibilities in the course of a new culture and civilisation upon the earth. In his lecture of 25 June 1908, in the cycle *The Apocalypse of St. John*, Rudolf Steiner says:

> True Anthroposophy can only put forward as the final goal the community of free and independent egos, of egos which have become individualized. It is just this that is the mission of the earth, which is expressed in love—that egos learn to confront one another freely. Love is not perfect if it proceeds from coercion, from people being chained together, but only when each 'I' is so free and independent that it does not have to love, when its love is an entirely free gift. It is the divine plan to make this 'I' so independent that as an individual being, in all freedom, it can offer love even to God. It would amount to man being led by apron-strings of dependence if he could in any way be forced to love, even if only in the slightest degree. Thus the 'I' will be the pledge for the highest goal of man. But at the same time, if it does not discover love, if it hardens within itself, it is also the tempter that plunges him into the abyss. For it is what separates people from

one another which brings them to the great War of All against All, not only to the war of nation against nation.[57]

What protects us from falling into the abyss is the struggle for balance, for finding the point of equilibrium in our humanity which we can glimpse in the Christ being. This experience of the middle, balancing realm is at the same time a conscious experience of the threshold, the bridge between the sense and spiritual worlds.

> The highest that can be given to us is the message of Christ Jesus. We must take it up thoroughly, not merely with our understanding; we must take it into our innermost being, just as one takes nourishment into the physical body.[58]

What unites us in the Anthroposophical Society since the Christmas Foundation meeting is the great common task of helping to awaken a consciousness in modern human beings of the threshold to the spiritual world, so that increasing numbers of individuals come to self-awareness and gain a connection to the great goals and tasks of humanity's evolution. This can only succeed, however, if we recognise the social edifice that Rudolf Steiner was able to found before his death—the Anthroposophical Society and the School of Spiritual Science with its various sections; if we recognise this great social edifice as something that can be realized only if human beings will it in the sense of the new Mysteries, experiencing themselves as building stones that help to create this social organism. The impulse of the new Mysteries can take hold wherever communities are successfully built in harmony with these ideals of humanity's future. The extent of the undertaking—of 'social building' extending far into the future—appears in a still broader dimension of co-responsibility for the future if we take into account Rudolf Steiner's statements of 5 August 1908. In this lecture, he describes how the Indian, the

Persian, the Egypto-Babylonian and the Greek cultural epochs were, at the same time, repetitions of the great stages of earth evolution. He describes how, in the Indian cultural epoch, the knowledge focused in the Mysteries mirrored what had been reality in the Polaric phase of earth evolution. The Mystery knowledge of the priests in the Persian epoch mirrored what had lived in the Hyperborean time of earth evolution. In Egypto-Babylonian culture was reflected the Lemurian time — the division of the sexes and the implantation of the ego in humanity's evolution. And in the Greco-Roman period the actual events of Atlantean times, and the gods, were mirrored in the knowledge of the mystery priests.

Building on this foundation, Rudolf Steiner continues:

> In our age of civilisation, the fifth, we have nothing to repeat. Let us bring this thought before our minds: we have nothing to repeat, no ancient remembrances. We have given birth to a fifth age of civilisation, one whose results will be seen in the future, while the four previous ages were repetitions of the four preceding cosmic epochs. Our age must give birth not merely to an ancient wisdom, but to a new wisdom, a wisdom which points not only to the past, but which must work prophetically — apocalyptically — into the future. In the Mysteries of past ages of civilisation we see an ancient wisdom preserved, but our wisdom must be an apocalyptic wisdom, the seed for which must be sown by us. Once again we have need of a principle of initiation so that the primeval connection with spiritual worlds may be renewed.
>
> The task of the Anthroposophical movement is to supply this principle. No wonder that wisdom has been lost to so many, for without the principle of initiation it is very difficult nowadays to obtain wisdom, more difficult than formerly, when the memory of ancient experiences had only to be refreshed, and when the results of earlier

development could be brought to human consciousness. Today this is difficult; therefore we can understand that the sense-world seems to be without God, and to be barren and empty; but although it appears as if the ancient spirit world had died out, it is there; it is working and fructifying, and if man wills he can find connection with the spiritual world.

Precisely at the moment when ancient memories seemed to be disappearing during the Graeco-Roman age, care was taken that a wonderful new seed for all future time should be laid within the cold ground of the earth; this seed is what we describe as the Christ-Principle. The apocalyptic wisdom, the true new spiritual wisdom, will be found in conjunction with this Christ-Principle, which does not point back only to memories of past epochs, but prophetically forward to the future; and precisely through this it summons us to action, to creative work.[...] Thus we see the connection between the past and the future, a future which already lies before us today as a field needing our work and endeavour.[59]

From what has been described here, two things can become clear. Firstly, that this new Mystery culture will arise out of quite different conditions from those of the old. What in the old Mysteries emanated from single, blessed people can only realise itself now 'when many unite at the right time'. Secondly, the principle of secrecy which was a central aspect of guarding ancient Mystery wisdom must give way to quite different conditions in the new Mysteries. For the central element of the new Mysteries is something which no power in the world can betray — because it is not dependent upon a particular kind of knowledge. The crucial thing now is solely whether the good is willed and done. And if it is done, then it reveals itself to the world through the doing, and has no need of secrecy. Modern times will not allow knowledge to be withheld anymore. Also, the individual ego has come to a stage in its development when it can and must learn to decide for itself what knowledge content it wants to open itself to, and from what it wants to close itself off. Silence and secrecy always existed in the first instance to safeguard those who were not yet ready, for, in order to be understood at all and to be assimilated positively, the real truths require a certain maturity in a person's development. Nowadays however, each individual wants to decide things for himself. No one is allowed to decide for someone else, even if error and guilt are the consequence of an unripe decision. In the new Mysteries, silence or secrecy is much more an aim of the will, a means by which meditative power can be concentrated so that a person can focus their strength and become more effective.

If we then examine Ita Wegman's question about a Mystery medicine against this background, it becomes clear which guiding orientations must be involved here. Firstly, a medicine that—as Rudolf Steiner already formulated in the fourth lecture of the first course to doctors—'... has the whole well-being of humanity in view',[60] and is not satisfied with looking only at the health and illness of separate individuals. Secondly, such medicine has to do with Mysteries of action and deed, to which the courage for healing and the unconquerable 'Karma Will', as Rudolf Steiner describes it in his lectures to young doctors, point the way. The third basic orientation becomes clear if we look at the example of the collaboration between Rudolf Steiner and Ita Wegman, which finds expression in the book they wrote together, *Extending Practical Medicine*, as well as in the many joint case-conferences. The Mysteries of the Will are, at the same time, the Mysteries of working together. Working together in this sense becomes possible to the extent that people are able to decide to place their lives and destiny in the service of the tasks of the future. This is the third great challenge which comes to meet the pupil of the renewed Mysteries.

2
The Evolution of the Medical Section in Connection with the School of Spiritual Science at the Goetheanum

At the Christmas Foundation meeting of 1923/4, Rudolf Steiner described the structure of the Anthroposophical Society and the School of Spiritual Science in connection with discussions being held about the society's statutes. In doing so, he showed four superimposed levels: Anthroposophical Society, First Class, Second Class and Third Class of the School of Spiritual Science. These levels — of the Society and the School — were then interwoven by the Sections, with their spiritual and cultural impulses. He sketched these relationships on the blackboard to help clarify this[1] (see diagram on p. 45)

From this drawing by Rudolf Steiner, it can be seen that the new impulse which the Esoteric School received at the Christmas Foundation meeting is closely connected with the founding of the Sections. For these did not yet exist in the old Esoteric School,[2] which existed from 1902-1914. Also there were no Sections connected with the cultic knowledge work[3] that similarly carried on from 1905/6 until the beginning of the war and was partially taken up afterwards again, ending only in 1921. In addition, neither esoteric school was open to the public. Personal invitation to join the work was needed. But once the School of Spiritual Science had been newly founded at the Christmas Foundation meeting, the Sections were inseparably linked with open, public work. For the Sections do not only have to fulfil their tasks within the School and the Society, but, as can be seen from the drawing, in public life as well. What is worked out here in the School will enter into common culture and take effect. The esoteric should place itself into modern culture, to renew civilisation and transform it. It should no longer lead a secret, hidden existence, for this derived from the stern rules of ancient Mystery centres that were separate from so-called exoteric life. The new form, which we must still learn to properly grasp, stands in the public domain and is subject to laws that are valid for the Mysteries of the Will, for the Mysteries of the future.

What is needed now, therefore, is to put into practice in the different spheres of life all that has been developed at various levels of the School and the Society. Every member is called upon to become a collaborator in one or other of these great cultural impulses, sketched here in the vertical lines of the drawing. And then Section work can take place on all levels of the Society and School—yes, and go further, into general human life itself, where collaborative work within institutions allows meetings to take place with people from a broader sphere. In the work of each Section therefore, there is always a natural tension between inner deepening of knowledge and outer working; just as Ita Wegman herself describes in her own work, and as we also experience daily when we meet the demands placed on us by our times, and when we feel the powerlessness of not actually being adequate for them.

Thus the Medical Section can only be seen as something that is evolving. The task was given and the goals are there to point us in the right direction. Now everything depends on what individual people, alone and in cooperative working, can contribute to the fulfilment of this task. What will happen is what we can decide to do, and—*what we will*. Upon this will also depends whether what Ita Wegman describes in her letter of 16 January 1935 to Franz Löffler[4] can come about. She wrote this when the leadership battles within the Anthroposophical Society had reached their peak:

When I returned from my illness, I thought for a long time about what could still be made out of this desperate anthroposophical situation, and the solution seemed to me to be the following: the Christmas Foundation meeting no longer functions in its totality, but the fact remains — whether one wants to recognise it or not — that the members of the Vorstand, connected to Dr. Steiner by a ceremonial act, have work to undertake within the Anthroposophical Society. Work for which they are responsible. If the work is done in the correct manner, as Rudolf Steiner wanted it to be, and those people who are bound to this work through destiny also co-operate and really take care that things can unfold correctly, then a time will come, despite all the difficulties, when unity arises again, even if it may perhaps be in the next life.[5]

On 27 September 1935 — the expulsion of Ita Wegman and Elisabeth Vreede[6] from the Vorstand had been passed by the members' meeting of 14 April 1935 — Ita Wegman warmly greeted the doctors who had come for the annual autumn conference in the Arlesheim Clinic, and then described the situation of the Sections thus:

If one has received a task from Rudolf Steiner, then it cannot be undermined. For it is there, no one can take it away, and one cannot separate oneself from it either. It is there once and for all. If difficulties now arise because people have come to see in a different light the tasks given to particular individuals by Rudolf Steiner, that is not proof that someone who was given the task should give it up. On the contrary, those who received the tasks must stick with them inwardly, strictly, steadfastly, taking it upon themselves to work further, with all their strength — even if it is not yet sufficient — on these tasks that were given to them. That is why I have taken it upon myself to continue, with those doctors who wish to work with me, the work that was started by Rudolf Steiner;

with all my strength but also, I would like to say, humbly. There is nothing else but to start again in a small way, yet still with what Rudolf Steiner laid as a seed in our hearts. And if one has once connected oneself to Rudolf Steiner then, as you all know my dear friends, no power in the world can do anything to dissolve the connection to this human being who has given something very great to the world. The work that is to be done here, which really should have been carried out together with Rudolf Steiner, has naturally become something quite different. But even though it has become something quite different, the warmth that we carry for it in our hearts is, and remains, the same. And so it must be understood; and so also must you connect yourselves, if you can, with what we wish to achieve here. If now — and this should stay within this small circle — we do not have the place that we really should in the Goetheanum, we are still working for the Goetheanum because we cannot separate ourselves from Rudolf Steiner. That goes without saying. We cannot separate ourselves from his work. In the spiritual Goetheanum all human beings have a place. It is necessary that I make my point of view clear, as this is the first time that we meet together after all the unhappy and difficult events, which for my part I look on as great misunderstandings, and which I hope will one day resolve themselves; so that the time may come in which we will be able to work together again with love and in peace.[7]

The work of the Medical Section has continued to the present day in harmony with these words — even if in a different form to the original intention. When Albert Steffen[8] called the close colleagues of Ita Wegman — Margarete Kirchner-Bockholt[9] and Madeleine van Deventer,[10] as well as Hans Bleiker[11] and Gerhard Schmidt[12] — to the Goetheanum in 1955 to form a 'College' that was to work towards re-enlivening the Medical Section at the Goetheanum, work could once again begin within the physical Goetheanum, as had been intended by the founding impulse of the Christmas Foundation meeting. With the start of the pastoral medical work in particular, the first seeds were laid in the Goetheanum to allow the original intentions to live anew. This goal of a re-enlivening of the original impulses was followed by later Section leaders, Margarete Kirchner-Bockholt, Walter Holtzapfel and Friedrich Lorenz, so that in 1991 there was a deep desire, particularly among German doctors, to hold the seventieth anniversary celebrations of the founding of both the clinical therapeutic institutions — in Arlesheim and Stuttgart — as an internal celebration within the School of Spiritual Science at the Goetheanum. That this was carried out and willed by the whole medical movement was shown by the lively visit of nearly 1000 people from 26 countries. And it speaks for itself that representatives of all the therapeutic professions, inspired by this event, for the first time gathered together in the Great Hall of the Goetheanum. Two years have passed since then, and this year we celebrate the 72nd anniversary of the founding of the present Ita Wegman Clinic and the Stuttgart Institute from which the Filderklinik is descended. I would therefore like to close these thoughts and stimuli for work, which have been gathered in this book in connection with this commemorative conference, with the hope that these observations will prove supportive and helpful to the further flourishing of the Medical Section. As a spiritual meeting place within the School of Spiritual Science, it has the task of building community in such a way that new possibilities for research can arise through collaborative work. Community building, however, is not only a question of knowing about a common ideal. Community building is, above all, a question of will.

Notes

GA = Rudolf Steiner *Gesamtausgabe*, the collected works of Rudolf Steiner in the original German, published by Rudolf Steiner Verlag, Dornach, Switzerland.

(The works of Rudolf Steiner in English translation are available from Rudolf Steiner Press, London, and Anthroposophic Press, New York.)

Foreword

1 The 'Freie Hochscule der Geisteswissenschaften'.

Part 1: Chapter 1 (pages 3–16)

1 This title is a quote from Rudolf Steiner's book *How To Know Higher Worlds*, New York 1994.
2 Ita Wegman, 1876–1943, was appointed by Rudolf Steiner to be the first leader of the Medical Section in 1924.
Cf Rudolf Steiner/Ita Wegman: *Extending Practical Medicine*, London 1996. M.P. Van Deventer: *Die anthroposophisch-medizinische Bewegung in den verschiedenen Etappen*, Dornach 1992. Hans Müller-Wiedemann: *Karl König*, Stuttgart 1992. J.E. Zeylmans van Emmichoven: *Wer war Ita Wegman*, Vol. I–III, Heidelberg 1990, 1992.
3 Rudolf Steiner: *Theosophy of the Rosicrucian*, London 1966.
Manifestations of Karma, London 1995.
Curative Education, Bristol 1993.
4 Rudolf Steiner: *Wiederverkörperung. Zur Idee von Reinkarnation und Karma* ('the idea of reincarnation and karma'), Stuttgart 1992. Emil Bock: *Wiederholte Erdenleben* ('repeated earthly lives'), Stuttgart 1981. Friedrich Husemann: *Vom Bild und Sinn des Todes* ('the image and purpose of death'), Stuttgart 1977.

5 Rudolf Steiner: *Between Death and Rebirth*, London 1975.
6 Rudolf Steiner: *The Christmas Conference for the Foundation of the General Anthroposophical Society 1923/24*, London/New York 1990.
7 Parzival, who undergoes a path of schooling, is the central character in a book of the same name by the medieval author Wolfram von Eschenbach.
8 Rudolf Steiner: *Theosophy*, New York 1994.
9 Rudolf Steiner: *Occult Science*, London 1969.
10 See note 1.

Part 1: Chapter 2 (pages 17–33)

1 Rudolf Steiner: lecture of 7.7.24 from *Curative Education Course*, Bristol 1993.
2 Novalis: *Hymns to the Night, IV*. Translated by G. Macdonald, London 1992.
3 Rudolf Steiner: *Discussions with Teachers*, New York 1997, and *Education for Adolescence*, New York 1996.
4 'Das Gute tun wollen' in German, which can mean both willing and wanting. (Translator's note.)
5 St Mark's Gospel, 10, 17–18.
6 Rudolf Steiner: *Pastoral Medical Course*, New York 1987.
7 See note 1.
8 The title of an Easter course for young doctors given in 1924.
9 Rudolf Steiner: *Theosophy of the Rosicrucian*, London 1966.
10 St Luke's Gospel, 6, 27–28: 'But I say unto you which hear, Love your enemies, do good to them which hate you. Bless them that curse you, and pray for them which despitefully use you.'

Part 1: Chapter 3 (pages 34–48)

1 Rudolf Steiner: *Drei Perspektive der Anthroposophie*, ('3 perspectives of anthroposophy') GA 225. Lecture of 15.7.23.
2 Rudolf Steiner: *The Work of the Angels in Man's Astral Body*, London 1988.

3 German poet of the Middle Ages and author of *Parzival*. His portrayal of a path of schooling in the pictorial imagery of that time still has vivid immediacy and relevance for modern readers.
4 Rudolf Steiner: *The Foundation Stone*, London 1996.
5 See *The Christmas Conference for the Foundation of the General Anthroposophical Society 1923/24*, London/New York 1990.
6 Rudolf Steiner: *Four Mystery Dramas*, London 1997.
7 German: Der Weltenbau muss werden
   Aus Menschen muss er erbaut werden
8 Rudolf Grosse: *The Christmas Foundation*, N. Vancouver 1984. F.W. Zeylmans van Emmichoven: *The Foundation Stone*, London 1996.
   Rudolf Steiner: *Die Konstitution der Allgemeinen Anthroposophischen Gesellschaft und der Freien Hochschule für Geisteswissenschaft. Der Wiederaufbau des Goetheanum* ('the constitution of the General Anthroposophical Society...), GA 260a.
   The verse by Steiner, translated by J.M. Josephson, is from: *Zur Geschichte und aus den Inhalten der erkenntniskultischen Abteilung der Esoterischen Schule von 1904 bis 1914* ('from the history and content of the knowledge and cultic section of the esoteric school from 1904 to 1914'), GA 265, 1987.

Part 2: Chapter 1 (pages 51–102)

1 Rudolf Steiner: *The Threshold of the Spiritual World*, London 1990. *How To Know Higher Worlds*, New York 1994.
2 Cf *Theosophy*, New York, 1994.
3 E.g. Rudolf Steiner: *Occult Science – An Outline*, London 1969.
4 Rudolf Steiner: *Awakening to Community*, New York 1974.
5 Rudolf Steiner: *Philosophy, Cosmology and Religion*, New York 1984.
6 Rudolf Steiner: *Spiritual-Scientific Aspects of Therapy*, GA 313. Lecture of 11.4.1921 (published by the Association of Anthroposophical Doctors).

Rudolf Steiner: *Anthroposophical Leading Thoughts*, London 1985.
7 Rudolf Steiner and Ita Wegman: *Extending Practical Medicine*, London 1986.
8 Rudolf Steiner: *Grundlinien einer Erkenntnistheorie der Goetheschen Weltanschauung, mit besonderer Rücksicht auf Schiller*, ('theory of knowledge based on Goethe's world conception, with particular reference to Schiller') GA 2.
9 Marie Steiner, 1867–1948, the wife of Rudolf Steiner, was given the task of overseeing the publication of his lectures and written works.
10 Rudolf Steiner: *Welt, Erde und Mensch* ('universe, earth and man'), GA 105. The English edition, *Universe, Earth and Man*, London 1987, does not include Marie Steiner's Foreword.
11 Cf Rudolf Steiner: *Occult Science – An Outline*.
12 See note 10. Lecture of 5.8.1908 in Stuttgart.
13 Cf Robert Ader et al.: *Psychoneuroimmunology*. San Diego, California USA, 1991
  N. Plotnikoff et al.: *Stress and Immunity*, Boca Raton, Florida USA, 1992.
14 See note 7, chapter 1.
15 Cf Rudolf Steiner: *Die Brücke zwischen der Weltgeistigkeit und dem Physischen des Menschen* ('the bridge between universal spirituality and the human physical constitution'), GA 202.
16 See note 12.
17 Rudolf Steiner: *Physiologisch-Therapeutisches auf Grundlage der Geisteswissenschaft. Zur Therapie und Hygiene* ('physiology and therapy on a spiritual-scientific foundation. On therapy and hygiene'), GA 314. Lecture of 7 April 1920.
18 Rudolf Steiner: *Die soziale Grundforderung unserer Zeit* ('the social requirements of our time'), GA 186. See also: Walter Holzapfel: *Auf dem Wege zum Hygienischen Okkultismus* ('on the path to hygienic occultism'), Dornach 1988.
19 See note 18. Lecture of 1.12.1918.
20 Rudolf Steiner: *Curative Education*. Bristol 1993.
21 Rudolf Steiner: *Theosophy of the Rosicrucian*, London 1996.
22 Cf Eberhard Amelung: *Ethisches Denken in der Medizin*,

('ethical thinking in medicine') Heidelberg 1992; F.J Illhardt: *Medizinische Ethik*, ('medical ethics') Berlin, Heidelberg, New York, Tokyo 1985.
23 Cf Rudolf Steiner: *Theosophy*.
24 Rudolf Steiner: *Anthroposophische Menschenerkenntnis und Medizin* ('anthroposophical knowledge of man and medicine'), GA 319.
25 Published in *Renaissance, Magazin der Transplantation*, Sitten, April 1993.
26 Lecture of 19.11.22 from: *Geistige Zusammenhänge in der Gestaltung des menschlichen Organismus*, GA 218.
27 Rudolf Steiner: *Anthroposophical Leading Thoughts*, nos. 35-37.
28 Cf Rudolf Steiner: *The Case for Anthroposophy*, London 1970.
29 Rudolf Steiner: *Theosophy*. Chapter 3, 'The Three Worlds'.
30 Rudolf Steiner: *Between Death and Rebirth*, London 1975.
31 Ibid.
32 See note 26.
33 At the time this was published, the abortion laws in Germany were being redrafted. This stimulated public debate and raised the whole issue into people's consciousness.
34 Glückler/Schily/Debus: *Lebenschutz und Gewissensentscheidung* ('protecting life and making decisions of conscience'), Stuttgart 1992; Friedwart Husemann: *Ethischer Individualismus und Schwangerschaftsabbruch* ('ethical individualism and pregnancy termination'), in *Das Goetheanum*, 13/199; Werner Hassauer: *Freiheit und Notwendigkeit beim Schwangerschaftsabbruch* ('freedom and neccessity in pregnancy termination') in *Das Goetheanum*, 31/32, 1992.
35 Rudolf Steiner: *Die Verantwortung des Menschen für die Weltentwicklung* ('human responsibility for world evolution'), GA 203. Lecture of 13.3.1921.
36 Frits Wilmar (1915-1992) was a Dutch doctor living in Germany
37 Frits Wilmar: *Vorgeburtliche Menschwerdung*, Stuttgart 1991.
38 ibid.
39 Max Hofmeister, a German embryologist.
40 Max Hofmeister: *Die Übersinnliche Vorbereitung der Inkarnation* ('the supersensible preparation for incarnation'), Basel 1979.

41 Author's italics.
42 Rudolf Steiner: *Meditative Betrachtungen und Anleitungen zur Vertiefung der Heilkunst* ('meditative observations and suggestions for a deepening of the art of healing'). First circular letter (Rundbrief) of 11.3.1924, GA 316.
43 Cf Rudolf Steiner: *Manifestations of Karma*, London 1995.
44 See note 40, p. 127.
45 See note 35.
46 Rudolf Steiner: *Geisteswissenschaftliche Behandlung sozialer und pädagogischer Fragen* ('a spiritual-scientific approach to social and pedagogic questions'), GA 192. Lecture of 1 May 1919.
47 ibid.
48 ibid.
49 J.E. Zeylmans van Emmichoven: *Wer war Ita Wegman*, ('who was Ita Wegman?'), Vol. 2, Heidelberg 1992.
50 ibid. Notebook 57.
51 ibid.
52 Rudolf Steiner: *The Apocalypse of St. John*, London 1985. Lecture of 17.6.1908.
53 Johann Wolfgang von Goethe: *The Green Snake and the Beautiful Lily*.
54 Rudolf Steiner: *Zur Geschichte and aus den Inhalten der ersten Abteilung der Esoterischen Scule 1904–1914* ('the history and content of the first section of the esoteric school, 1904–1919'), GA 264. See the address given on 15.12.1911 in Berlin.
55 See note 49.
56 Rudolf Steiner: *Influences of Lucifer and Ahriman*, New York 1993; Rudolf Steiner: *Cosmic Memory*, New York 1990. In the Bible, Diabolos (Lucifer) and Satanas (Ahriman) are spoken of.
57 See note 52. Lecture of 25.6.1908.
58 Ibid.
59 Rudolf Steiner: *Universe, Earth and Man*, London 1987. Lecture of 5.8.1908.
60 Rudolf Steiner: *Geisteswissenschaft und Medizin* ('spiritual science and medicine'), GA 312. Lecture of 24.3.1920 in Dornach.

Part 2: Chapter 2 (pages 103–107)

1. Rudolf Steiner: *The Christmas Conference for the Foundation of the General Anthroposophical Society 1923/1924*, London/New York 1990.
2. Cf Rudolf Steiner: *Zur Geschichte und aus den Inhalten der ersten Abteilung der Esoterischen Schule* ('the history and contents of the first section of the esoteric school'), GA 264.
3. Cf Rudolf Steiner: *Zur Geschichte und aus den Inhalten der erkenntniskultischen Abteilung der Esoterischen Schule* ('the history and contents of the cultic knowledge section of the esoteric school'), GA 265.
4. Frans Löffler was leader of the Curative Educational Institute in Gerswald near Berlin, and one of the founding curative educationalists. He was a close colleague of Ita Wegman, and had a particular love for the whole field of curative education.
5. J.E. Zeylmans van Emichoven: *Wer war Ita Wegman?* ('who was Ita Wegman?'). Vol. 3, Heidelberg 1992.
6. Elisabeth Vreede, 1879–1943, was a member of the original Vorstand (Executive Committee) and leader of the Mathematical and Astronomical Section at the Goetheanum.
7. See note 5. Author's italics.
8. Albert Steffen (1885–1963) was an original member of the Vorstand, and after Steiner's death became its leader.
9. Margarete Kirchner-Bockholt, a close colleague of Ita Wegman and one of her three trustees. She pioneered curative eurythmy and was a leader of the Medical Section.
10. Madeleine Deventer (1899–1983) was another close colleague and trustee of Ita Wegman. She was one of the original group of medical students who asked Rudolf Steiner to give the course later known as the 'Young Doctors' Course'.
11. Hans Bleiker was an early anthroposophical doctor who was asked to help heal the divisions within the medical movement.
12. Gerhard Schmidt was also an early anthroposophical doctor invited to help heal the divisions.